COMMUNITY SELF-HELP HOUSING MANUAL:
PARTNERSHIP IN ACTION
Revised Edition

Robert William Stevens
Ted Swisher, Editors

Intermediate Technology Development Group
of
North America, Inc.
1986

© 1986 by Habitat for Humanity, Inc.
All rights reserved.

ISBN 0-942850-05-X

Published for Habitat for Humanity, Inc. by
the Intermediate Technology Development Group
of North America, Inc.

Cover design: Elizabeth Sheehan
Photo credits: Habitat for Humanity, Inc.

Printed in the United States of America

Habitat for Humanity
Habitat and Church Streets
Americus, Georgia 31790-3498
(912/924-6935)

Intermediate Technology Development
Group of North America, Inc.
P.O. Box 337
Croton-on-Hudson, New York 10520
(914/271-6500)

CONTENTS

HABITAT FACT SHEET   v

ACKNOWLEDGMENTS   vii

CHAPTER I: THIS IS HABITAT

    A Brief History   1
    Rationale   7
    Habitat Visions   8

CHAPTER II: BASIC POLICY

    The Habitat Covenant   23
    Affiliate Tithing (Policy Statement, April 1985)   26
    Government Funds   29
    Sweat Equity   30

CHAPTER III: GETTING STARTED

    Assessment of Needs   33
    Front-End Notes   34
    Some Thoughts from Established Projects   37
    Inflation   38
    Volunteers--An Important Resource   39
    Nashville Area Habitat's Approach   40
    Habitat Resource Materials   45

CHAPTER IV: BASIC COMMITTEES

    The Board of Directors   47
    The Site Selection Committee   49
    The Family Selection Committee   51
    The Building Committee   63
    The Fundraising Committee   66
    Other Committees   69

CHAPTER V: ORGANIZATIONAL REQUIREMENTS

Becoming an Affiliate	73
Legal Incorporation	74
Tax-Exempt Status	75
Documents Needed to Sell a House	76
Delinquent Payments	77
The Habitat Covenant: Basic Document	79
Sample Completed Affiliate Application of Northeast Mississippi Habitat for Humanity	82
Excerpts from Articles of Incorporation and By-Laws	91

APPENDIX A: COMPLETE LISTING OF MATERIALS AVAILABLE THROUGH HABITAT 93

APPENDIX B: SAMPLE HOUSE PLANS 97

APPENDIX C: FURTHER SOURCES OF INFORMATION ON LOW-COST, ENERGY-EFFICIENT HOUSING 101

DIRECT CREDITS 112

HABITAT FACT SHEET

HABITAT FOR HUMANITY

building houses in partnership with God's people in need

WHO CONTROLS AND MANAGES HABITAT FOR HUMANITIY?
An ecumenical Board of Directors of 25 persons meets semi-annually to determine policy and oversee operations. In conjunction with a larger Board of Advisors (150 members), they pledge to support administrative costs, so that money contributed by you goes directly into serving needy people. Heavily dependent on volunteer labor, the Americus headquarters currently operates with nine salaried administrative staff persons (Executive Director, Administrative Director, Director of Operations, Director of Volunteer Services, Affiliate Project Coordinator, Media Director, Director of Development, and two International Project Coordinators), a salaried bookkeeper, and a small paid clerical staff.

IS HABITAT INCORPORATED?
Yes. Incorporated as a tax-exempt, non-profit organization. All contributions are tax-deductible.

HOW IS HABITAT FOR HUMANITY FUNDED?
Money comes from gifts and non-interest loans from individuals, churches and other organizations who are moved by concern and compassion to lend a hand to those in need. New homeowners are encouraged, as well, to contribute what they can in addition to their regular monthly house payments so they, too, can help others have decent housing as they have been helped.

HOW MUCH DO THE HOUSES COST? HOW LONG DO PEOPLE HAVE TO PAY?
Differences in location, labor, land and material costs lead to a wide margin in cost factors. Currently, a house in Africa costs $2,000-$2,500; in Guatemala, $1,500; in Haiti, $1,250; in Peru, $3,000; in Nicaragua, Bolivia, and India, $1,000; and in the U.S. the average is $25,000. Mortgages, on a no profit, no interest basis, are over a 20 year period. Many, if able, choose to pay them off in a shorter time.

HOW ARE PEOPLE CHOSEN TO HAVE A NEW HOUSE?
A committee in each location reviews the hundreds of applications. Financial need is primary, but this is a loan program and other factors such as ability to pay, size of family, character...are taken into consideration. All projects use basically the same guidelines for such decisions.

WHAT IS THE DIFFERENCE BETWEEN A SPONSORED AND AFFILIATED PROJECT?
All sponsored projects are, at present, outside the U.S. Sponsorship means that Habitat takes full responsibility for funding and securing of personnel for the project. An affiliated project, on the other hand, is responsible for its own fundraising, local promotion, staff, etc. They are, however, entitled to use the Habitat name, to advisory counsel and assistance, and to help from the Americus staff.

---

419 West Church Street, Americus, Georgia 31709 (912) 924-6935

The Habitat for Humanity newsletter, Habitat Happenings, and newspaper, Habitat World, serve as conduits of information and communication for all projects. This helps generate funds and volunteers for all projects. Gifts received by the Americus office, designated for a specific project, are forwarded to that project, affiliated as well as sponsored.

HOW DOES A HABITAT FOR HUMANITY PROJECT GET STARTED?
This varies from area to area. Generally, if you see a need in your area, think the concept is feasible and there is a group of dedicated Christian people willing to explore the possibility, simply contact the Americus office, expressing your interest, and things will happen from there. Often Habitat can plug into an already existing program.

HOW CAN I BECOME A VOLUNTEER?
Contact the Habitat office in Americus for a volunteer application. We need volunteers to work in the U.S. projects, for a day, week, month, two years. You can help with construction or office related work. We also need volunteers to serve overseas, making at least a three year commitment including a period of training in Americus.

IF I CAN'T SPEND TIME AT ANY OF THE PROJECTS, HOW ELSE CAN I HELP?
Use your imagination! Spread the word...give a slide presentation...raise money...distribute Habitat literature to people in your neighborhood and church...sell or give Bokotola and Love in the Mortar Joints to friends (one pastor in New York sold over 1,500 copies of Bokotola and over 700 copies of Love in the Mortar Joints)...get articles about Habitat printed in your local newspaper. And, of course, you can send a check either as a gift or as a non-interest loan. All gifts are tax-deductible. Come - - be a partner with us and with God in this new mission frontier!

Recommended Reading:

#83105   Cotton Patch Evidence by Dallas Lee ($3.50) The story of Clarence Jordan and Koinonia Farm, where Habitat for Humanity was born.

#83100   Bokotola by Millard Fuller ($4.95) The story of the first housing project in Zaire, and the events leading to the creation of Habitat for Humanity.

#83101   Love in the Mortar Joints by Millard Fuller and Diane Scott ($4.95) The more complete story of Millard Fuller's personal pilgrimage and the remarkable ministry of Habitat for Humanity.

Audio Cassettes:

#83020 "The Economics of Jesus" - Millard Fuller ($3.50)
#83019 "Envisioning" - David Rowe ($3.50)

Audio/Visual Presentations:

#83006 "Love in the Mortar Joints - II" Slide/Tape Program ($25.00)
#84100 "WORLD IN NEED...Opportunity to Share" VHS Video Cassette ($25.00)
#84101 "WORLD IN NEED...Opportunity to Share" Beta Video Cassette ($25.00)
#84200 "Shelter of God's Love" 16mm Film, 44 min. ($35.00 two-day rental)
        "Shelter of God's Love" also for sale as VHS or Beta Video Cassettes

A catalog, Sharing the Vision, containing all of the Habitat materials is available upon request. All of these materials can be ordered through Habitat for Humanity.

ACKNOWLEDGMENTS

The *Community Self-Help Housing Manual* grows directly out of the experience of Habitat for Humanity and the people involved in its program of self-help housing for low-income persons.

Credit for the first edition goes first to Habitat affiliate project leaders who have worked through the formation and development of their own affiliate projects, second to John Dorean and Jerry McFarland who brought a mountain of material together, third to Bill Givens who extracted and compiled a first-round manual, and finally to Bob Stevens who amplified, consolidated, and edited the original "How To Manual," based upon his experience with project leaders.

This revised edition also includes contributions from such volunteers as Tom Brooks of Nashville Habitat, Kathy Dupont from Laconia Habitat on "Volunteers," Dan Rhema from Chesapeake Habitat on "Site Selection," and Mary Lyons Barrett from Omaha Habitat who helped work through many of the revisions. Affiliate Coordinator Ted Swisher used the first edition over the past four years, then collaborated with Bob Stevens to bring about this revised *Community Self-Help Housing Manual*, personally contributing several of the new sections.

In addition, this revised edition of the *Manual* includes an expanded Chapter I, explaining the religious and philosophical basis of Habitat for Humanity--for it is that religious basis that forms the "motor" behind the Habitat movement. A new Chapter II develops the overall operational philosophy of Habitat for Humanity.

Millard Fuller, the co-founder of Habitat for Humanity, was partly responsible for Chapter IV on organizational requirements. Harry Sangree, a former Habitat volunteer and current trustee of the Intermediate Technology Development Group of North America, wrote the brief history of Habitat in Chapter I. Ward Morehouse, chairman of ITDG/North America, contributed to the overall editing and especially the section on energy-efficient building techniques in Chapter IV. Cynthia Morehouse, ITDG publications editor, was responsible for copy editing and production supervision, as well as contributions to the sources of further information in Appendix C. Special thanks also should go to Elizabeth Sheehan who donated her time in redesigning the cover for this edition.

In short, preparation and publication of this *Manual* was--like community-based self-help housing for low-income people must be--a cooperative endeavor in which many took part.

CHAPTER I: THIS IS HABITAT

A BRIEF HISTORY

Habitat for Humanity has built hundreds of homes for thousands of people. It builds simple houses and sells them at cost, with no interest, to people who otherwise couldn't own their own home. Habitat builds to "provide a decent house in a decent community for God's people in need." The group is a growing social and spiritual movement creating tangible results that affect people's lives. Today, it reflects many contributions of varied talents and gifts. But as recently as the late 1960s, Habitat for Humanity was little more than an exciting idea in the minds of two unusual men: the late Clarence Jordan and Millard Fuller.

Clarence Jordan was one of the co-founders in 1942 of Koinonia Farm, a cooperative Christian community which still exists near the small southern Georgia town of Americus. Jordan was a trained farmer and a Biblical scholar. The farm served as a springboard for his belief that Christianity requires a social conscience as well as a spiritual dimension. His stalwart belief that race does not divide men in God's sight made him a target of violence that reduced the once-thriving community to two tired couples looking for new directions in their lives. The darkest time was the summer of 1968.

Concurrently, Millard Fuller was making his way to a creative rendezvous with Jordan. Raised in rural Alabama, Fuller became active in church organizations and involved in various entrepreneurial ventures. He attended college and continued his education at law school, starting a successful mail-order business during his law school days. Fuller had that amazing ability to apply enormous personal energy to significantly modify an existing situation. Before the age of 30 he was worth over $1 million. Then his life fell apart. His marriage was decaying, his health was failing, and he felt far apart from the religious moorings of his youth. Fuller decided to liquidate his assets and give them away, and then directed his considerable talents to raising $10 million for Tougaloo College, a small Black institution in Mississippi. After launching a successful fund drive, Fuller and his family went to Koinonia Farm to consider the next step in their lives. The time was the summer of 1968.

Fuller and Jordan came together at this significant time in both of their lives and created the framework for today's Habitat for Humanity. An open letter to the friends of Koinonia Farm told of the new future for Koinonia:

> We have the deep feeling that modern man's greatest problems stem from his loss of any sense of meaningful participation with God in His purposes for mankind. For most people God really and truly is dead, stone dead.... It has also become clear that man has lost his identity with his fellow man. We compete with one another fiercely; we even want to kill. Our cities provide us anonymity, not community. Instead of partners, we are aliens and strangers.[1]

Steps to respond to these problems included "partnership housing" implemented through a Fund for Humanity.

> What the poor need is not charity but capital, not caseworkers but co-workers. And what the rich need is a wise, honorable and just way of divesting themselves of their overabundance. The Fund for Humanity will meet both of these needs.
> Money for the Fund will come from shared gifts by those who feel they have more than they need and from non-interest bearing loans from those who cannot afford to make a gift but who do want to provide working capital for the disinherited.... The Fund will provide working capital for the disinherited. It will provide capital for the...[housing construction].
> The...[involved beneficiaries] will be strongly encouraged, though not required, to contribute as liberally as possible to the Fund so as to keep enlarging it and making more capital available to others.... If the partners have the right spirit (and I cannot see how this or any other system can work without that) and there should be a growing number--which seems reasonable to predict --the Fund will be self-generative and ever-expanding.[2]

In 1968, Koinonia laid out 42 half-acre sites with four acres in the center reserved as a community park and recreational area. The idea of the Fund for Humanity excited people, and capital from all over the country arrived to start the work. After Jordan's death in late 1969, Fuller continued leadership of the project. The Fund for Humanity built four-bedroom homes with bath, kitchen, and living room and sold them to families at no cost and no interest. As the partner families paid their flat monthly fees (on the 20-year loan), capital was freed for houses for others. All new owners were encouraged to share at least part of their savings on interest with the Fund for Humanity for, "even

---

[1]Cited in Millard Fuller, *Bokotola* (New York: Association Press, 1977), pp. 17-18.
[2]Ibid., pp. 18-19.

the poorest should not be denied the extra blessedness of giving."

The original project was completed in mid-1972 and a new phase was laid out and begun. After almost four years at this, Fuller was restless to try something new. He had often wondered if the idea of a Fund for Humanity would function in developing countries. In 1973, at the invitation of the Church of Christ of Zaire and under the sponsorship of the Christian Church (Disciples of Christ) in the United States, he and his family traveled to Mbandaka, Zaire (formerly the Belgian Congo). They worked with church officials in Equator Region to create a Fund for Humanity, and began constructing houses, selecting families, and educating the community on the responsibilities involved with such a venture.

Although the road was far from easy, success did come. With the help of the local church and government, the interest of most of the community, and financial support from U.S. churches, the Fullers created a community out of a swamp. Two thousand people are now housed in solid concrete block homes with dry floors and strong roofs.

After the Fullers returned to the United States, the idea continued to flourish in Zaire. Projects range in size from the upgrading of parts of large cities to the complete reconstruction of entire villages, so that everyone acquires a new home. A major transformation is taking place.

In September of 1976, Fuller called together a group of committed Christians to discuss the future. Habitat for Humanity as an organization was born at this meeting. It would "always be thoroughly ecumenical.... It would remain a low-overhead operation, financed at each location by a revolving Fund for Humanity...[and] it would serve as a facilitating group, linking resources with people in need through existing [institutional] structures."[3]

Since Habitat for Humanity was created, it has exploded. In fiscal 1984, just eight years after its formal incorporation, $1.6 million in gifts passed through Habitat's Americus headquarters, and another $1.9 million went directly to U.S. affiliated programs. Its Board of Directors and Advisors total over 190. Nine paid staff members at headquarters and hundreds of volunteers perform all types of work to accomplish its corporate vision.

There are two distinct types of Habitat projects: sponsored and affiliated. A sponsored project (usually in a developing country) is one to which Habitat for Humanity commits funding and the provision of personnel. By spring 1985, there were 24 sponsored projects in 13 countries, with additional serious interest shown from Tanzania, Ghana, Colombia, other areas of Haiti, and the Solomon Islands.

An affiliated project is one which uses the Habitat name and abides by its guidelines, but is responsible for generating its own funds and recruiting its own personnel through a local Board of Directors.

---

[3]Millard Fuller and Diane Scott, *Love in the Mortar Joints* (Chicago: Follett Publishing Company, 1980), p. 82.

One hundred and fifteen established affiliated projects in 36 states exist in the U.S. as of October 1985.

Many more are on the horizon. A summary of project results is shown in Table 1 (and accompanying Figure 1) on the following pages. Current housing prices range from $1,000 for a two-room house in Alto Beni, Bolivia; Aguacatan, Guatemala; Khamman, India; and Herman Pomares, Nicaragua, to an average of $24,000 in the U.S., depending upon the lot price and the size of the house.

The story of a Habitat project, sponsored or affiliated, is always the same. People are enthusiastic about this successful approach to a significant social problem. They come from varied backgrounds but they have one goal--to improve and go through the steps outlined in this *Manual*. The results have been remarkable. Some photographic proof follows this chapter.

This *Manual* does not attempt to tell the full story of Habitat for Humanity, only to transmit the experience Habitat has gathered in its first nine years. Information on its organization, its history, and its people can be found in the following books:

Bokotola by Millard Fuller. (1977) $4.95
> An account of the first housing project in Zaire, and the events leading to the creation of Habitat for Humanity.

Cotton Patch Evidence by Dallas Lee. (1971) $3.50
> The story of Clarence Jordan and Koinonia Farm, where Habitat for Humanity was born.

Kingdom Building: Essays from the Grassroots of Habitat edited by David Johnson Rowe and Robert William Stevens. (1984) $4.95
> In-depth essays from the experience of Habitat partners--for leaders of local projects.

Love in the Mortar Joints by Millard Fuller and Diane Scott. (1980) $4.95
> The more complete story of Fuller's personal pilgrimage and the remarkable ministry of Habitat for Humanity up to the present time.

No More Shacks! by Millard Fuller. (forthcoming early 1986)
> The continuing story of Habitat for Humanity and its campaign to eliminate poverty housing.

These books and answers to any particular questions are available from:

Habitat for Humanity, Inc.
Habitat and Church Streets
Americus, Georgia 31709-3498
912/924-6935

TABLE 1

U.S. Affiliated Projects as of Fall 1985*

ALABAMA
  Shoals (Florence)
ARIZONA
  Tucson
CALIFORNIA
  Contra Costa County
    (Martinez)
  Fresno
  Sacramento
  San Joaquin County
    (Stockton)
  Sonoma County
    (Santa Rosa)
COLORADO
  Denver
CONNECTICUT
  Greater Bridgeport
FLORIDA
  Broward County
    (Fort Lauderdale)
  Immokalee
  Lee County
    (Fort Myers)
  Manasota
    (Sarasota)
  Pensacola
  Pinellas
    (St. Petersburg)
  Tallahassee
GEORGIA
  Americus
  Atlanta
  Cartersville/Bartow
    County
  Coastal Empire
    (Savannah)
  Columbus Area
  Monroe County
    (Forsyth)
  North Central
    Georgia (Ellijay)
  Northeast Georgia
    (Clarksville)
  Peach Area
    (Fort Valley)
  Rome/Floyd County
  Thomasville/Thomas
    County
ILLINOIS
  East St. Louis
  McLean County
    (Bloomington)
  Metro-Chicago
  West Garfield
INDIANA
  Boone County
    (Lebanon)
  Evansville
  Lafayette

KANSAS
  Topeka
KENTUCKY
  Ashland-Ironton Area
  Paducah
  Woodford (Midway/
    Woodford County)
LOUISIANA
  Covington
  Lafayette Parish**
  New Orleans Area
MAINE
  Greater Portland
  York County
    (Ogunquit)
MARYLAND
  Chesapeake
    (Baltimore)
  Garrett County
    (Oakland)
  Montgomery County
    (Rockville)
MASSACHUSETTS
  Beverly
  Boston
  Greater Lawrence
  Worcester
MICHIGAN
  Grand Rapids
  Kalamazoo Valley
  Lake County (Baldwin)
  Muskegon County
    Cooperating
    Churches
    (Muskegon)
MINNESOTA
  Twin Cities
    (Minneapolis)
MISSISSIPPI
  Coahoma**
  Friars Point**
  Holmes County
    (Lexington)
  John's Development
    (Prentiss)
  Jonestown**
  Mississippi Delta
    (Sumner/Tallahatchie
    County)
  Northeast Mississippi
    (Tupelo)
MISSOURI
  Kansas City
  Missouri (Hayti)
NEBRASKA
  Omaha
NEW HAMPSHIRE
  Lakes Region
    (Laconia)

Merrimack (Warner)
NEW JERSEY
  Jersey City
  Paterson
  Salem County
    (Woodstown)
NEW YORK
  Buffalo
  Cazenovia Area
  Flower City
    (Rochester)
  Lower East Side
    (New York City)
  Mid-Hudson Valley
    (Poughkeepsie)
  North Country
    (Malone/Franklin
    County)
  Syracuse
NORTH CAROLINA
  Catawba Valley
    (Hickory/Catawba
    County)
  Charlotte
  Forsyth County
    (Winston-Salem)
  Heart of Carolina
    (Raleigh/Wake
    County)
  Orange County
    (Chapel Hill)
  Statesville-Iredell
    (Statesville)
  Thermal Belt (Tryon)
  Transylvania (Pisgah
    Forest/Transylvania
    County)
  Western North
    Carolina (Asheville/
    Swannanoa)
OHIO
  Ashland-Ironton Area
    (Ashland, KY/
    Ironton, OH)
  Dayton
  Trumbull County
    (Warren)
  Zanesville
OKLAHOMA
  Enid
OREGON
  Portland
PENNSYLVANIA
  Greater Philadelphia
  Greene County
    (Jefferson)
  Tri-County
    Pennsylvania (State
    College)
  York
SOUTH CAROLINA
  Central South

Carolina (Cayce/
  Columbia)
Greenville County
  (Greenville)
Pickens (Clemson/
  Pickens County)
Sea Island
  (Johns Island)
TENNESSEE
  Appalachia (Robbins)
  Holston (Kingsport)
  Knoxville
  Mid-South (Memphis)
  Nashville Area
TEXAS
  Amarillo
  Austin
  Beaumont
  Dallas
  Longview
  San Antonio
UTAH
  Box Elder County
    (Brigham City)
VERMONT
  Green Mountain
    (Burlington)
VIRGINIA
  New River Valley
    (Christiansburg)
  Peninsula
    (Newport News)
WASHINGTON
  Buena Partners
  Tacoma/Pierce County
WISCONSIN
  Milwaukee
  Southwest Wisconsin
    (Dodgeville)
SPECIAL AFFILIATE
  Milledgeville, GA -
    Habitat for
    Handicapped
    Humanity
REGIONAL/NATIONAL
  CENTERS
  Habitat West -
    Santa Cruz, CA
  Rocky Mountain
    Habitat -
    Boulder, CO
  Habitat Mid-West -
    Clarendon Hills, IL
  Habitat of the
    Ozarks -
    Springfield, MO
  Habitat Northeast -
    Acton, MA
  Habitat South -
    Tupelo, MS
  Habitat of Canada -
    Thornhill, Ontario

Total of houses completed (1976-1984)   160
Total of repairs made in same period   308

*For a current listing of projects, contact the Affiliate Coordinator's Office in Americus.
**Provisional projects.

FIGURE 1

(Numbers indicate cumulative totals at each year's end.)

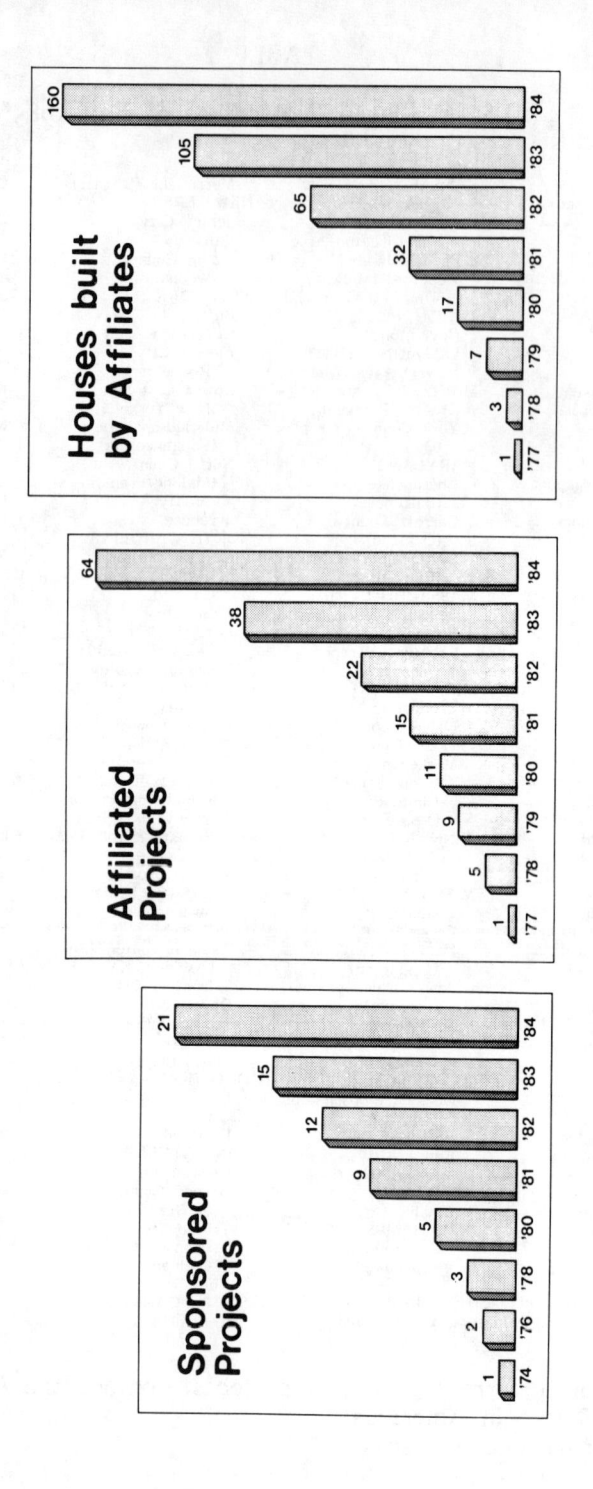

RATIONALE

Habitat's basic foundation for ministry is compassion, concern, and love. Habitat is based on the conviction that Christian discipleship must be lived out in practical ways which will help to lift burdens from the shoulders of others, especially those of God's people, who, for various reasons, need such help.

Since housing is a fundamental need of humanity, housing is the area in which Habitat's efforts are centered. The motto of Habitat is, "A decent house in a decent community for God's people in need."

Habitat is not a give-away program, but a joint venture where those who benefit from the housing ministry are involved at various levels in the work. Some people help with the actual construction of their houses and help their neighbors with theirs. Contributions sometimes are made by people in one project to those in another. All of this is based on the concept of partnership. "The poor need capital, not charity; co-workers, not case workers." Habitat also stresses the concept of people caring for others in the community. More than houses are involved. In the African projects, there are churches, schools, medical clinics, parks, and small backyard businesses, all of which contribute to a sense of community among the people in the houses.

The overall results of Habitat's work are matters of faith. Based on what is called the "Economics of Jesus," Habitat seeks to take what is available, offer it to Christ to help meet human need, and trust the results to God. Succinctly put, the Economics of Jesus state that God will multiply the minute to accomplish the gigantic when Christians, by sharing and sacrifice, focus upon human need in the name of Christ and not upon some humanly created standard of merit. Human life, no matter how insignificant it may seem, is priceless. With such a focus in Jesus' name, He will multiply financial resources to accomplish the gigantic. Believers and persons of good will join such efforts in an everwidening circle of participation. In doing so, they will recognize the truth in what Jesus said: "It is more blessed to give than to receive."

The Economics of Jesus, applied to Habitat for Humanity, take the very specific form of stepping out on faith to build houses at no interest and no profit to sell to poor folks. Small beginnings, dedicated in the name of God to the service of needy brothers and sisters, will be multiplied bountifully by Him. As the affluent participate in such a program, they come to realize the truth in the statement by Ethel Dunning, homeowner at Koinonia in Georgia: "There ain't no way you can live in big houses with lots of money and plenty of food and they is po' folks all around you livin' in shacks and hongry and God is gonna be happy with you."[4]

---

[4]Millard Fuller and Diane Scott, op. cit., p. 96.

Our philosophy of ministry has two basic features. First, we require that those who qualify to purchase a Habitat house must be in need of a decent house, and they must be unable to purchase a house through conventional methods. Second, there is no interest, profit, or finance charge involved. This philosophy comes from the original Koinonia Partners' housing program which was designed to benefit low-income rural families in southwest Georgia.

Habitat affiliates do not use any public tax money for construction. Affiliates are encouraged though to cooperate with city and local government and become familiar with other area public and private housing organizations.

To begin a successful local Habitat project, there must be at least one person who shares the vision and understands the operating principles of this ministry, and who can recruit others to join in a venture of faith in that local area.

Further, it is strongly urged of the people who might be serving on new local boards and committees that they read especially two books listed in the previous introduction about Habitat: Millard Fuller and Diane Scott's *Love in the Mortar Joints* and *Kingdom Building* edited by David Rowe and Bob Stevens.

Some of the affiliated projects have been fortunate enough to have an individual who is supported financially through a volunteer service program or denominational agency. That person is approved by his church agency to work in a Habitat project. In forming a local board to begin a project, it would be good to contact various churches in the area to see if such a sponsorship through a denominational agency is possible. A number of Christian agencies are involved at various levels in housing programs.

Every major Protestant denomination, as well as Roman Catholics, support Habitat by either sponsoring volunteers or contributing financially to an affiliate. As affiliates spring up in more and diverse locations, there will be an even stronger ecumenical base on which Habitat will build. Besides denominational agencies, those involved in starting up an affiliate should also try to draw into the affiliate any area interdenominational groups that might already be involved in housing. Contacting such local groups can bring other resources into the program.

HABITAT VISIONS

The tenth chapter of Acts records the visions received by Peter and Cornelius. Cornelius is instructed to send for Peter in order to have Peter explain the Good News to him. Peter is instructed to do the precedent-breaking job of taking the Good News to a Gentile. That incident was the turning point in taking the Gospel to the non-Jewish world. Peter received many objections from the Apostles for his action; yet, he defended his action as the will of God revealed in his vision from God. He supported his belief by telling the Apostles what happened when he did carry the message to Cornelius.

The vision we have at Habitat for Humanity is the vision of a decent house in a decent community for God's people in need. The sale of these houses at cost with no profit and no added interest is a vital part of that vision. Included in the vision is a strong emphasis on local decision making in each project. The incidents surrounding Peter's vision and Cornelius' vision may be instructive for us as we seek to carry out the Habitat vision. Let us declare, as did Paul before King Agrippa, that, "we have not been disobedient to the heavenly vision" (Acts 26:19).[5]

The Biblical Experience

The first thing we notice is that the vision was born in prayer and meditation. There is no substitute for this reflective groundwork. Also, we notice that Cornelius was afraid and Peter protested at the force of the vision--very much in accord with human nature. Cornelius was overwhelmed; Peter saw it as something different from what he had previously understood. Confronted with our tasks, we often respond similarly.

Despite their feelings, both Peter and Cornelius responded immediately to their God-given vision. Their intermediaries, the persons Cornelius sent, and the main characters--Peter and Cornelius-- were ordinary people like you and me, but they were empowered by the vision. We are called to act swiftly on the vision we have or we may lose it.

Note, too, that the vision occurred only once. Peter did not receive several visions telling him to take the Good News to the Gentiles. He received it only once but acted upon it the rest of his life. History tells us that he acted on it so wholeheartedly that many years later he was crucified on a cross in Rome, choosing to be crucified upside-down because he was not worthy to be crucified in the manner of his Lord. Most of us do not expect to be crucified (or even die for the faith in any manner). But we may well expect opposition, even from good Christian brothers and sisters, just as Peter received objections from the other Apostles. We must hold to our vision as Peter held to his.

The vision may come only once; yet, we are to act upon that vision the rest of our lives. The vision is something general, broadly directing our lives. Its details are "fleshed out" over time by the many people we meet and the many circumstances we are in. We may even be led through difficult situations and conflicts, but as these are

---

[5]All scripture references have been taken from the Revised Standard Version of the Bible.

resolved we grow in our understanding of the vision. We are in Habitat for the long haul, for it is only over the long haul that we can significantly affect the capital-intensive housing needs of God's people in need.

Before going on to specific elements of our Habitat vision, we will look at another valuable section in the story about Peter and Cornelius. Peter's sermon summarizes the life and message of Jesus (Acts 10:34-43). That message was the Good News of peace preached by Jesus of Nazareth who was anointed with the Holy Spirit and with power. He went about doing good and healing all who were oppressed by evil. Today, more than ever, do we need people anointed with the Spirit and power, going about doing good and creatively liberating those oppressed. We must reflect that in our life today those principalities and powers, which we call by different names, do rule our world, sometimes even over those who call themselves Christians.

A Ministry to the Rich as Well as the Poor

Habitat for Humanity is a two-pronged ministry--to the poor and to the affluent. The ministry to the poor is the most obvious. We seek to provide capital, not charity, and co-workers, not caseworkers; for it has been our experience that if the poor are given the opportunity to obtain a decent house, they will work hard to overcome their substandard living situation. Since we provide the capital for a decent house with no profit and no interest, we attempt to relieve the poor of the heavy burdens that keep them from owning good housing. The houses are priced within the income range of the poor so that the actual cost of the house does not become a burden on their backs.

In the Gospel, we read that God causes the sun to shine and the rain to fall on all persons--the good, the bad; the just, the unjust; parents and children; men and women--and, in fact, we read that the good news of the Gospel was sent to all persons. Thus, the principal criterion for receiving a Habitat house is need--presently living in a bad house in a lousy living situation. Religion, race, color, kinship, friendship are not criteria which determine whether one gets a house; only need does. We try to put into practice Emperor Julian's description of Christians (circa 362 AD) when he tried to stimulate a pagan revival in the Greek religion. Said Julian to the pagan priests, "We must learn from the Christians, who take care not only of their poor, but our poor too." That really tells us something about Christianity at the climax of one of its most dynamic eras.

The second prong of Habitat's ministry is not as obvious to the affluent. The Fund for Humanity[6] is designed to be a wise, just, and

---

[6]The Fund for Humanity is the name given in every project site to the fund of money used to build houses. The Fund's money comes from contributions of organizations, churches, and individuals of good

honorable way by which the affluent may divest themselves of some of their affluence. Both the affluent and the poor are joined together in partnership through the Fund for Humanity. It is the vehicle through which the poor obtain capital for their homes. The Fund for Humanity is also the vehicle by which the affluent are challenged to divest themselves of some of their affluence in a (hopefully) wise and just way. The partnership through the Fund for Humanity ties the poor and the affluent together in a relationship similar to that admonished by the Apostle Paul in II Corinthians 8:13-15. The words of James and John further strengthen this side of the ministry. James tells us that even the devils have faith, and that what is needed is good works, since one's faith is completed by his works (James 2:18-22). John asks us the poignant question: "If one has the world's goods and sees a brother in need, yet closes his heart against him, how does God's love abide in him?" (John 3:17). The ministry of Habitat for Humanity relates closely to the ministry of Jesus and the early church.

No matter which way we look at our modern affluence and the standard of living to which we have so grown accustomed, when we compare it to what Jesus called riches, we see that the vast majority of contemporary American Christians are rich. It just may be that our affluence is a spiritual liability in much the same way possessions were to the rich young ruler Jesus talked with (Matthew 19:16-26). The young ruler had kept all the commandments, possibly even better than do most church-going Christians today. The scriptures tell us Jesus loved him, but the young ruler went away saddened, for his riches stood in the way of his spiritual growth. We in Habitat do not ask people to give away all they have and live in poverty. We affirm the goodness of what God has blessed us with. Yet, we believe that our affluence may be the spiritual liability that prevents the camel from going through the proverbial eye of the needle (Matthew 19:24). The Fund for Humanity provides the mechanism for us to divest ourselves of some of that affluence so that we may live more simply and others may simply live. We challenge people to give to the Fund for Humanity and/or to tithe their house payments.

Paul asked the Christians to share their abundance to help supply the want of others that there might be some type of equality (II Corinthians 8). Paul added that he did not want them to be burdened while others were eased. He likened the process to when God gave the Israelites the manna in the wilderness: "He who gathered much had nothing over and he who gathered little had no lack" (II Corinthians 8:15). We remember what happened to the manna when it was stored. Maggots grew in it even the next day. Could it be likewise that God has showered us with our affluence, but if we hoard it, spiritual maggots will grow in it? Could it be that our affluence is also meant to be shared? This understanding of the two-pronged ministry of

---

will, from no-interest loans to the Fund, from income from project enterprises, and from Habitat house payments.

Habitat for Humanity is certainly part of the vision.

Christian Partnership

Because of this vision of life and discipleship, our lives take on a relationship that we call partnership. It is through this partnership that we come to see ourselves as co-workers, not case workers; that we come to work together with all people as brothers and sisters. One does not dominate the other, but each one works with one another on an equal footing, each contributing from his or her experience and expertise for the good of all.

This sense of partnership includes volunteerism. If a highly motivated person comes to us saying he wants to work as a volunteer, a partner, or a co-worker in a Habitat project, we have always accepted that person as a partner. At times, this has been for a two- or-three-year term; at other times, a shorter term of a couple of months or weeks. These partners work in the Americus office, overseas, and with U.S. affiliates. They go out as brothers and sisters, as co-workers who work side by side with other Habitat workers. This, too, becomes not only a ministry to those receiving houses, but also a ministry to the volunteer and to her or his home congregation.

Volunteers often return to their home community with new insight about justice, Christian living, simplicity, service, and Christian responsibility. To one extent or another, volunteers returning to home communities become "conscientized" to become ambassadors for spreading the good news of the Kingdom of God. To be sure, this is an idealized version of what happens, but it is included in the vision. The vision of partnership causes ripples in ways we may not know.

As part of the vision of partnership, we come to feel a strong solidarity and kinship with brothers and sisters who earn two or three dollars a day--if and when they can find work. Regardless of the country, that is not enough to live on. We become partners in the venture which helps bring better housing in a dignified way to other partners. Their needs become part of our needs; their pains, ours.

Thus, the vision is expanded beyond ourselves, our family, even our local Habitat project to become one with those who throughout the world are also struggling to provide decent housing for themselves or others. This serves to move the vision beyond even an expanded self-interest in our own area to include a vision for the people of the world.

As the vision expands, we are also sensitized to see the need of changing our own lifestyle and witness. We see that our over-consumptive lifestyle is in part tied to our partner's under-consumption. We begin changing our ways, thus becoming more moral members of the Christian and world communities.

In this partnership, the poor are also challenged to participate in many ways. They may help, or may be required to help, in the construction of their house or a neighbor's house. They may serve on a local Habitat committee and/or help reduce the bundles of paperwork that pass through the local Habitat office. Furthermore, recipient families are challenged to make direct contributions and repay their loan at a faster rate so that their funds may be used even earlier for the building of another Habitat house.

Living the Vision

As Christians, we are called to be other than a reflection of our culture. In the field of housing and in the use of money, we believe that Habitat is on the cutting edge where our culture has no solutions. We must remain faithful to the vision so that we may find solutions. Our commitment to charge no interest is a very important decision in making the kind of change necessary in enabling the poor of the world to attain a decent level of living. This idea is very old and it is Biblical. We do not try to "proof text" our efforts; yet, we do believe that this idea has a solid scriptural basis. In Exodus 22:25, we read: "If you lend money to any of my people with you who are poor, you shall not be to him as a creditor, you shall not exact interest from him." In the Bible, we see one who loans his/her money at interest as one who is ranked with the person who takes a bribe against the innocent (Psalms 15:5). And, we see that a prophetic righteousness is lending without interest (Ezekiel 18:5-9). How different this is from the viewpoint of our culture! As we remain faithful, we can help find solutions.

Habitat is also on the cutting edge of what is happening in low-income housing. People respond to our pleas for help daily. Our spirits join in affirming this witness to the Gospel and in affirming our common humanity in dealing with the problem of brothers and sisters living in wretched housing. People are saying, "no profit, no interest; yes, we agree with that idea." The time is right for this approach. The integrity and the dignity of homeownership, of paying for those costs that went into the building of "my" house (at no profit and no interest), even for the poor, is an idea whose time has come--as also have come the applied concepts of partnership, and of co-workers, not case workers. People all over are joining in affirming the ideas of partnership and being co-workers in providing a decent house in a decent community for God's people in need.

We know that the time for these ideas has arrived as we read our mail and receive contributions each day. Many of the contributions represent real sacrifice. Others ask how "we" ("they," "us," as we are partners in the vision and the work) can start a Habitat project in such diverse locations as Bridgeport, Connecticut; Albuquerque, New Mexico; or Fort Wayne, Indiana. People are taking seriously the idea of incarnational evangelism in ministering to all of God's people--the poor and the affluent--as we make concrete the claims of the Gospel.

We persist in our prayer that Habitat for Humanity continues to be a movement of God whose time has come. We persist in attempting to live the vision.

Above: Setting roof trusses on a concrete block house in Immokalee, Florida.
Below: Volunteers at Johns Island, South Carolina nail roof decking on a donated panelized redwood house.

An attractive house renovated by Portland (Oregon) Habitat for Humanity.

Ada and Eva Goad and Mark Frey stand on the front porch of the Goad's new house and look at their old house in the foreground.

Three houses built by Kansas City Habitat. The homes were designed to blend with older houses in the neighborhood.

Above: Jimmy Carter helps to frame a house in Americus, Georgia.
Below: Solar house built by Habitat affiliate in Tryon, North Carolina. This same design has been utilized by the Asheville project. A concrete slab stores heat and the total cost was only slightly more than a similar house with a conventional heating system.

This six-story, 19-unit tenement was completely rehabilitated by Habitat for Humanity on the Lower East Side of New York City. The families who live in the building are organized as a cooperative.

An attractive sign is displayed at most Habitat construction sites. A telephone number is helpful for those who may want to support the program.

Sandra Graham and Mrs. Viola Allen stand in front of Viola's house --a combination which renovated Viola's old house and constructed a new addition.

A Habitat house is not complete until it is dedicated. During the dedication of her house Dianne Ellis of Americus, Georgia jumps for joy in front of her new house.

The new (almost completed) and the old in Ntondo, Zaire. This too is part of the worldwide scope of Habitat for Humanity.

A community park in Mbandaka, Zaire is part of "a decent house in a decent community for God's people in need."

CHAPTER II: BASIC POLICY

THE HABITAT COVENANT

The Habitat Covenant is the basic policy statement of Habitat for Humanity's relationship with a Habitat project. This is the document around which a Habitat project functions. It is signed by the board of the local Habitat affiliate and by the International Board of Directors. The Covenant is a covenanted moral agreement between the two boards. Each agrees to operate by the principles of the Covenant.

The Habitat Covenant is a moral and spiritual document, not a legal document. From a Christian/moral perspective then, this covenanted moral relationship is on a higher plane than a legal relationship. It requires more than a legal relationship. The Covenant is drawn from the broad basis of the Christian faith, not something imposed from the outside. Rather, it is a statement of faith and policy that is drawn from our Biblical faith. It is a statement mutually agreed upon by the two Habitat boards rather than imposed upon one board by the other. The Covenant then is a mutually agreed-upon statement of the principles and policies of Habitat, not foreign to our faith in God. Further, it is stated in such a way that it allows a large degree of freedom within the Habitat family.

There are several basic points contained in the Habitat Covenant. The first point is that all the work of the local Habitat program is to demonstrate the love of God in Jesus Christ. The local Habitat program is to be an outward expression of the love and mission of the church. Thus, as much as possible, the local Habitat program is to be connected to and related to the local church. Habitat, in fact, is to be a mission of the church, but definitely not *the* mission of the church. The distinction here is that there are many elements of mission which are to meet the physical, social, and spiritual needs of humankind. In Habitat's programs, Habitat seeks to meet the housing needs of "God's people in need." Of course, the local Habitat program works with the people it serves in other areas too, although the focus is always around their housing needs.

Second, the board of the local Habitat affiliate must be an ecumenical one, representing the various churches interested in cooperating in a local Habitat program to help improve the housing needs of low-income people. This ecumenical board should be composed of lay persons, as well as clergy, professionals, and low-income people, thus insuring a broad range of perspective and wisdom for a stronger base of operations. The locus of decision-making authority lies within the local board, as long as it operates within the broad framework of the Habitat Covenant. In focusing upon its ecumenical relationship, what we recognize is that although we may not agree in finer points of doctrine, we do agree in service in the name of our Faith.

The third point is that the houses should be built at no profit and sold at no interest. This is very vital. It is what people identify with when they talk about Habitat for Humanity. Building (or remodeling) houses at no profit and selling them at no interest is essential to the vision of Habitat. In the Old Testament Law (Exodus 22:25 and Leviticus 25:36), the scriptures say: "If you lend money to my people who are poor, do not be like a money lender, do not charge them interest." Psalm 15 begins by asking the question, "Who shall ascend the hill of the Lord, who may enter into His holy temple?." It answers that question in several ways, concluding with, "He who does not charge interest of the poor." What Habitat does from the basis of these scriptures is to say, "This is the path in which we choose to go." We are not saying that everybody should refuse to charge interest; we are only saying that we do not charge interest to the poor. In that sense, Habitat seeks to be very much of an alternative to our culture (Roman 12:1,2).

The fourth point of the Covenant is that in each local Habitat project there will be an objective, non-discriminatory selection process. This, too, is very important to the whole operation of Habitat. If there is discrimination or favoritism shown in the selection process, then those who are discriminated against may very legitimately ask the question, "How does such an action demonstrate the love of God?" Ephesians 2:14 says, "He [Christ] has broken down the dividing wall between us." The dividing wall at that time was between the Jew and Gentile. It was surely as rigid as the dividing wall between races in the United States. If that wall was broken down by Christ, certainly others were too. Furthermore, John 3:16 reads that, "God so loved the world..." So often, we skip over this verse not thinking that it means the *whole* world--not just the Christians, or Anglos, or Zairians, or short people or tall people. It means *all* people. As disciples of Christ, we also ought to demonstrate such a love and relationship for all people. Matthew, Chapter 5 indicates how God caused the sun to shine and the rain to fall on *all* people, not only the just people. Once again, that would admonish us to make Habitat housing available to all persons in a non-discriminatory manner.

Since the Habitat Covenant is a moral covenant, each local Habitat board morally commits itself to use an objective, non-discriminatory process of selecting families to receive houses. Habitat does not have a set of guidelines that says, "This is objective and non-discriminatory, and this is not." Rather, Habitat trusts the integrity of each local group to understand its local situation, then develop processes by which an objective, nondiscriminatory selection procedure will be employed. It is this moral accountability with the focus of decision-making power at the local level that is one of the important strong points of the whole Habitat relationship.

Fifth, the Covenant states that the Habitat houses shall be simple, decent houses, which are built within the socio-economic ability of the families to repay. This, too, is very important. The houses must be simple, within the cultural context of the local area. That means that Habitat housing in the United States currently (1983) ranges from 800 to 1,200 square feet, and in cost from about $12,000 to $35,000. The average Habitat house is probably in the low $20,000 range. In overseas programs, Habitat housing is considerably smaller in size and varies in cost from $800 for a small, decent two-room house with a large porch to about $3,000, depending upon various factors. It is equally important, in any case, that the house be built at a price and amenity level that is affordable by the Habitat family purchasing the house. Never does Habitat want to put a heavier burden upon the family than it can bear. This is done through not charging interest on the house, and by building a very simple house.

The sixth point of the Covenant is the establishment of a revolving "Fund for Humanity." It is the Fund for Humanity which is the resource base for each program. Mortgage repayments always go back into the local Fund for Humanity and are recirculated to build more houses. The Fund for Humanity is an open system. The local Habitat group continues to seek additional sources of funds to enter the local Fund. That way more and more houses can continue to be built through the Fund for Humanity. If a local project is ever completed, and there are no more houses that need to be built in a local area, the local Habitat board commits itself to send the incoming funds from its local Fund for Humanity to be used in another local Fund. One of the purposes of the Fund for Humanity is well stated in the initial letter which Clarence Jordan and Millard Fuller sent out to prospective persons in the launching of the Koinonia Fund for Humanity. The Fund was designed to be, "a wise, honorable and just way of divesting themselves [the affluent] of their overabundance...."[7] That speaks for itself.

The seventh and final major point of the Habitat Covenant is that each Habitat affiliate shall have its books audited annually, and that they shall be open and available for review by anyone. This is good business practice and maintains the integrity and public confidence in a local program. Nothing should be hidden. All that a local affiliate does should be shouted from the house top! In a study Millard Fuller did on legal ethics, he concluded that not only should one avoid evil, one should also avoid the appearance of evil. How much more should this be the case of a local Habitat board, for even any suggestions of

---

[7]Millard Fuller and Diane Scott, op. cit., p. 18.

this be the case of a local Habitat board, for even any suggestions of wrongdoing could be very detrimental to what Habitat truly seeks to do.

Anything that does not contradict the above principles of Habitat, as developed in the Covenant, is a field open to the local discretion and decision making of the local Habitat board. That is the power of the Habitat movement. Local people have within their hands the decision-making authority for their own program. There are no national or international guidelines which determine local policy. Rather, there are mutually agreed-upon principles that arise directly out of the implementation of the Christian faith in the local program. Such is the commitment made in the signing of the Covenant by the board of the local Habitat affiliate and by the International Board of Directors of Habitat for Humanity.

AFFILIATE TITHING (POLICY STATEMENT, April 1985)

Over the past year or so, the issue of affiliated projects tithing to the international program has been a very troublesome one. Each U.S. affiliated project struggles to obtain its own funds to build homes in the local community. Thus, it feels a very strong "stewardship" of those funds for helping God's people in need in that community. Yet, Habitat is a worldwide movement which seeks to tie all people together, affluent and poor, in one effort to make an assault on a common cause--the elimination of poverty housing.

Out of this extensive discussion, the resolution is that AFFILIATE TITHING IS VOLUNTARY BUT EXPECTED. Habitat believes that affiliate tithing is an appropriate way to relate the affiliate program to Third World needs, expressing that spirit of global partnership so essential to Habitat's ministry. This approach is Biblical, challenging, exciting, and in keeping with the Habitat vision.

A Voluntary Relationship

One of the strongest principles of Habitat for Humanity is that Habitat is a voluntary association of persons gathered together to work toward the elimination of poverty housing. This is carried out on a very local level--in Kansas City, Tucson, Memphis, the Mississippi Delta, and many other places throughout the United States--as well as on an international level in Zambia, Zaire, Uganda, Kenya, Guatemala, Nicaragua, Peru, and other countries. All around the globe, rich, poor, and affluent are joining together via the Fund for Humanity, putting their hands to the hammer, combining their resources, in order to turn this dream into deed. For example, Kansas City partners have been able to say, "we are building houses in Kansas City, and Memphis, and Zaire, and Uganda." We are indeed co-workers with many others.

There is *no* financial requirement to join with Habitat in this international movement. Affiliate-related expenses incurred through the Americus office are offered as part of the larger effort to eliminate poverty housing from the face of the earth. However, with the proliferation of U.S. affiliated programs (as of October 1985, there are 115 established U.S. affiliates, with many more on the horizon), we have begun to realize that large sums of energy and funds may be redirected, without conscious intent, from the international programs to the local U.S. programs. For example, over the past year or two, much of Millard Fuller's time has been involved in speaking on behalf of the affiliated program. Thus, his energies, which would have gone for raising funds for the housing needs of brothers and sisters in developing countries, have instead been channeled for needs in the United States.

We also realize, however, that even the scarcity of income of an affiliated project, struggling to build simple houses at a minimum but adequate U.S. standard, is an abundance relative to the scarcity and poverty in which Habitat works overseas. Even a "tithe" of the cost of the average U.S. Habitat house builds one to two houses in a developing country. And, as we believe the truth of Acts 20:35 which quotes Jesus as saying, "It is more blessed to give than to receive," we realize that the abundance God has given us is meant to be shared with our needy brothers and sisters. It is our privilege to work to help others have a more decent physical environment in which to live.

A Biblical Basis of Partnership Giving

The following are a few Biblical passages pertinent to the issue of tithing. Second Corinthians, Chapters 8 and 9, have a lot to say about the issue of financial giving for the needs of others. We see from those chapters that giving is a voluntary act. Of their own free will, the Corinthians begged for the privilege of helping God's people in need. However, as St. Paul describes the needs of others, he indicates that he is not laying down rules that must be followed. Yet, the Apostle Paul goes on to say that the basis of giving is in the abiding abundance of our Lord Jesus Christ: "Rich as he was, he made himself poor for our sake, making us rich by means of his poverty."

The purpose of giving is not to relieve others by putting a burden on us. Rather, it has to do with fairness and equity, as the scriptures say, "that the one who gathered much did not have too much, and the one who gathered little did not have too little."

Chapter 9 concludes the discussion by saying that, "he who plants sparingly shall reap sparingly, and he who plants generously shall reap generously. Each should give not with regret out of a sense of duty, but out of the abundance of his heart." Finally, Paul says that, "God loves a cheerful giver."

We must keep focusing on the voluntary aspect of tithing, rather than making it a law. If we fail to do so, we must fall into the trap of Matthew 23:23 where Jesus indicates that the Pharisees tithed mint, dill, and cumin, but ignored the weightier matters of the law--justice, mercy, and faith. That our brothers and sisters in our country, and in overwhelming numbers overseas, must live in subhuman conditions is a terrible injustice that throws shame upon the message we preach about the love and mercy of God. However, as we seek to work together to try to relieve such conditions, both in our country and overseas, let us keep our efforts on a voluntary, positive relationship that flows out of abundance, and which responds to love, justice, and mercy. Let us not make the issue of tithing a legal one. In other words, tithing should be a joyful "want to," not a begrudging "have to."

The Expanse of Our Partnership

People in Guatemala have moved out of dirt-floor, cane-stalk houses (with polyethylene thrown around the cane to try to keep out the wind and cold) into decent, sturdy, earthquake-resistant houses. People in Nicaragua will be moving out of dirty, rat-infested, palm thatch lean-to's into decent, adequate housing. Families who suffered from some of the ravages of the Idi Amin regime in Uganda have moved into solid brick houses in Gulu, Uganda. The entire village of Ntondo in Zaire is being rebuilt under local leadership and with Habitat programs. Such spontaneous developments are part of the Habitat partnership all over the world.

The Habitat Board of Directors strongly urges the U.S.-affiliated projects to tithe their income for the needs of brothers and sisters in developing countries. Even though all of the affiliated programs are struggling to try to meet the needs of low-income families in their area, a tithe of that income will build even more houses for brothers and sisters overseas. It is just amazing that such small amounts can yield such an abundance. This is part of the miracle of being about His work and the multiplication of His fruit. As stated earlier, the adopted position is that *tithing is voluntary but expected.* It is expected (although not required) that affiliated programs share their resources with less advantaged Habitat programs in other countries, thus making the affiliates a part of real global partnership.

Many of the projects are adopting a "sister-sponsored project." Other U.S. projects are committing themselves to tithe their income, or to tithe each house that they build; to tithe house payments, or to support a Habitat volunteer in one of the overseas-sponsored programs. Specifics are determined by each project on a project-by-project basis. As this is done, that partnership solidarity grows and becomes a real part of a local program's ongoing efforts.

Conclusion

Habitat requires no membership fee or tax for an affiliate to become part of the international effort. It is a privilege to be so involved. However, Habitat very strongly urges a local affiliate to tie its success to the international program so as to share the tremendous abundance that God has so freely given us as North Americans. We are thus able to reach even less fortunate persons and families in other parts of God's world.

Tithing is a real expression of solidarity and partnership with people in the Third World. It is Habitat's "partnership" in its broadest context--beyond one's own project, one's own city, state, and even country. In a very real sense, it expresses the oneness of each and all of us under the creation of our Lord--Oh God, help us to generously share the first fruits of the abundance that you have so freely given us. . . . Amen.

GOVERNMENT FUNDS

> The Affiliate Covenant on page one states that:
>
> ... the overall project operation will be without interest and free of government control. Government funds will not be used to build Habitat houses. It is a people-to-people project of love under the lordship of Jesus Christ. However, streets, utilities, land, or old houses needing rehabilitation may be acquired from government agencies if no strings are attached that violate Habitat principles. That assumes that the Habitat concept is justifiable grounds for appeals for a stewardship response from Christians anywhere.

While this is Habitat's position, Habitat does not want to be arrogant or dogmatic about government funds. In our world today, there is no way that an organization can be totally removed from government involvement, and Habitat does not see this as a desirable position. There are very legitimate government responsibilities, such as streets, utilities, and sometimes even land. Habitat's decision against the direct use of government funds does not come from a belief that government is evil, but from a sense that Habitat has a unique prophetic role to fulfill: One's involvement in meeting the needs of brothers and sisters is a very integral part of the Gospel of Christ. Furthermore, as Habitat Board member Jimmy Carter has articulated, there are many good organizations in the country who accept government assistance and desperately need funds, and Habitat does not want to compete for these limited resources. Habitat has a different role in the area of housing as we appeal to churches and individuals to share with God's people in need in a voluntary, person-to-person relationship.

On a more pragmatic level, Habitat is concerned about dependency on such an unstable source of funds, and thus prefers to rely upon the more stable resources of the private sector. Even local governments are finding that there is little money available for building new low-income housing units. Habitat is also aware that government funds seldom come with no strings attached. Some organizations have accepted government funds under the assumption that they had fulfilled their obligations, only to find that a government audit, conducted a year or two later, required additional staff time to answer questions and come up with certain figures.

An organization in low-cost housing in Boston does not seek government funds because it has found that the value added by government participation is cancelled out by the cost incurred by government regulations.

Habitat is also concerned about the effect that government funding will have on homeowners and contributors. We do not want contributors to be overwhelmed (and driven away) by large government grants. We want homeowner families to participate in the Habitat ministry as partners by helping other families to obtain a decent house. We want the family to realize that the house was made possible by a caring and sharing of concerned individuals, and we are asking them to care and share as well.

SWEAT EQUITY

"Sweat equity," along with non-discriminatory, no-profit, no-interest sales of houses to low-income families, is a key characteristic of Habitat for Humanity. The new homeowner is expected to contribute his own sweat equity in the building of his house. This sweat equity, along with the volunteer labor of other Habitat partners, is an integral part of that which builds Habitat's solidarity across economic, class, racial, and national divisions. The Habitat Covenant states that sweat equity is to be an agreed-upon provision for a family to receive a house.

Sweat equity is the family's own unpaid labor that goes into the construction of their own home. It reduces the monetary cost of the house, but even more importantly, increases the family's personal stake in it and develops those lines of partnership with other persons. The amount and type of sweat equity varies from project to project and, to some extent, from family to family. It may be contributed by any member of the family--adults and children--with their hours being counted equally; it may have to do with picking up after skilled workers, performing administrative work, or working on the actual construction. Five hundred hours are required in Habitat houses built in Americus; this may be fulfilled through tasks, ranging from physically working on the house to helping collate the newsletter, *Habitat Happenings*. In many other U.S. projects across the country, sweat equity is held up as an ideal often, or "as much as is feasible." Usually, there is considerable effort made by the local Habitat board and leaders to motivate recipient families with regard to self-help, if that motivation is not already there.

The Chicago, Tucson, Charlotte, Tallahassee, Thermal Belt (North Carolina), and Omaha affiliates each require or strongly recommend between 250 and 500 hours of sweat equity. Acceptable types of sweat equity include helping with fundraising, office work, supplying lunches for the workers, cleaning, child care for other volunteers, painting/wallpapering, clearing weeds, landscaping, house watching, and actual renovative construction work. Tucson and Omaha keep records on the number of hours completed and, as an indication of the family's earnestness, ask potential homebuyers to put in some of their hours before they close on the house. Omaha allows the family to withdraw before closing on the house (up to 100 hours of the 500 hours required and reimburses the family for their work up to this point at the minimum wage). Omaha also allows families with small children or handicapped members to do office work in their own homes. Amarillo, on the other hand, has found that it is easier for the family to complete most of their required 200 hours after they have moved in, when logistics and work schedules are less of a problem. In Immokalee, families work 750 hours over two years from the date they are chosen. Any hours not completed by the end of the second year cost the family $4 an hour, payable in monthly installments. Some affiliates, such as Paducah and Coastal Empire (Georgia), while strongly recommending that homebuyers perform sweat equity, do not specify a set number of hours or keep records on the number of hours completed.

Some affiliates expect the homebuyer or a representative from the family to work on the house. For new affiliates, sweat equity requirements and provisions are in a learning stage, but will crystallize after the affiliates have had more experience in monitoring the work of prospective homebuyers.

CHAPTER III: GETTING STARTED

ASSESSMENT OF NEEDS

When one begins dreaming of a Habitat program and wishes to jump right into the construction of the first house, it seems that the front-end time going into a project is incredibly long. Yet, a long (but well-used) front-end period will vastly improve the transition from the early vision of a Habitat affiliate to its reality in the form of the first houses. Patience and hard work are the keys to developing a successful project.

One of the most important considerations related to the development of a Habitat project is the need for decent housing in a given area. Habitat wants to provide decent housing for people who are currently living in substandard housing. Habitat does not narrowly or rigidly define substandard housing because this will vary from one area of the country to another. For example, the lack of insulation may not make a house substandard in Georgia, but it would be totally unacceptable in northern Michigan.

You should have a good understanding of the housing needs in your area before starting a Habitat project. Talk to local officials, social workers, and ministers. Obtain statistics about the number of substandard units in your city or county. It is a good idea to visit a few needy families who might be interested in purchasing a Habitat house. If your research leads you to conclude that there is a need, then it will be easier to obtain support for Habitat as people realize that the committee has done its homework.

Habitat is not a program to provide the opportunity of homeownership for families who are already living in decent housing. At times, we may build for people who are living in a building that may not be substandard in a strict sense, but there are other circumstances that warrant Habitat involvement. For example, some public housing projects may have decent individual units, but the environment may be unacceptable. Habitat is flexible enough to make allowances for unusual circumstances.

If there is some need for decent housing in your area, but the need is not tremendous, you may want to form an affiliate that would donate half of its contributions to a sister project overseas. In this way, a group can be involved with Habitat and have a balanced program which supports a local project and the overseas ministry equally.

FRONT-END NOTES

If you do decide to organize an affiliate, there are a number of tasks you will need to carry out during the front-end time. *The first task is motivating people in your city or county.* Speak with as many people as possible on an informal basis. Then have a few general meetings (evenings or mealtimes) to begin to coalesce people around the Habitat vision in your area. If possible, have someone from the Americus office, a regional center, or one of the affiliated projects as guest speaker at some of these meetings. The dissemination of the books, *Love in the Mortar Joints, Bokotala, Kingdom Building,* and *No More Shacks!,* which tell the Habitat story--as well as the showing of the Habitat slide shows, videocassettes, and the film "Shelter of God's Love"--are all very helpful in this early stage as they help link your fledgling affiliate to an organization with an established track record. Other media productions are available from the Americus office together with other free literature, such as Habitat brochures, fact sheets, as well as the newsletter *Habitat Happenings* and newspaper *Habitat World.*

Following these meetings, a steering committee should be appointed which can report back to the general body. Its tasks should include the initial organization of the project, the formation of a Board of Directors, and so forth. The size of the Board of Directors should conform to the laws of your state. It is also good to support the Board of Directors with an auxiliary Board of Advisors of actively interested and supportive persons. There are many tasks included in getting a program going: publicity, public relations, administration, answering correspondence, legal matters, relations with municipal officials, and the like. In general, the broader the ecumenical base of these two boards, the more successful will be the project: housing construction is just too capital-intensive to be identified with only one church or denomination, regardless of how wealthy that church may be.

Is there an ecumenical umbrella agency, such as a council of ministers or service agency, under which the new Habitat program might function until the program establishes its own track record and obtains legal incorporation and tax-exempt status? This gives the local affiliate a way to begin raising funds while it is incorporating itself and obtaining its tax-exempt status. (Funds may also be held in escrow for the new affiliate at Habitat for Humanity's international headquarters in Americus, Georgia.)

Besides the promotional materials from the International Office, a new affiliate ought to develop its own brochure which states to the local community its philosophy, goals, and motivation. Keep materials as professional (although not slick) looking as possible. It is good to add to Habitat slide shows some slides which reflect local needs and the work of the local affiliate.

In addition, the local affiliate should begin developing its own mailing list and a periodic newsletter. With their permission, these individuals can also be added to the national mailing list, further enabling them to understand the Habitat vision. When speaking about Habitat, offer people the opportunity to sign up for the mailing list, but don't pass a paper around the room. Let the interested persons go to a designated table to give their names, thus pinpointing only the truly interested.

A very important administrative task (hopefully accomplished through volunteers) is a personal response to all contributions and inquiries. Personal contact is vital to this people-to-people ministry. Present contributors are the most probable source of future contributions. A prompt and personally written "thank you," plus a connection through the local and international newsletters, maintains that initial interest.

Somewhere in the early phase of affiliate organization, a team from the new affiliate ought to be sent to Americus or to an established affiliate. A firsthand visit is worth a thousand words. There, the team will see and feel the simplicity of the ideas and the objectives through concrete examples of decent housing in decent communities. Keep the Americus office and your regional center informed of your progress. It is a good idea to send board meeting minutes and relevant material to Americus as you develop your organization.

As you explore the possibility of forming an affiliate, it is important to be able to use the Habitat name. This is perfectly acceptable. However, please check with Americus before filing incorporation papers or printing materials under the Habitat name. Requests to use the Habitat name when filing incorporation papers should be made to the Americus office in writing; requests to use the Habitat name in printed material can be made by telephone.

If you are organizing yourself around the time of a Habitat International Board meeting (held in April and October each year in different locations around the country), it is worth the cost to send a leader from the local project to that meeting. There, these representatives will be able to experience the breadth and depth of Habitat and talk with affiliate leaders who have gone through similar efforts.

Fundraising is absolutely essential to such a capital-intensive ministry as housing. It might be that the new affiliate can find matching funds or seed monies from denominational sources that will challenge related individuals to contribute to the emerging project. The building and fundraising committees might also seek in-kind contributions such as materials, labor, and/or time. Churches can be challenged to put the new project in their monthly budgets. Individuals can be challenged to tithe their monthly house payments.

Speak about Habitat whenever and wherever possible: to church groups and committees, Sunday School classes, mission societies, civic groups, and individuals. Stress that the Habitat approach builds human dignity and self-reliance, independence and stability.

After a target area is selected, it is important to get to know people who live there. You need to understand their needs, feelings, goals. You need to listen to them as well as to acquaint them with Habitat philosophy. You will need a few sensitive volunteers who have that gift of easily establishing rapport with people.

These volunteers may work with house recipients to help pull together their downpayment, to help them budget to live within their restrictive incomes, to encourage them not to buy all new furniture when they move into their new homes, to facilitate contacts with public or private agencies which aid needy low-income families, and/or to serve as concerned individuals in time of need. All this must be done in the spirit of true friendship--not condescendingly as a kindly benefactor helping the needy, which will only lead to resentment.

It is always good to cultivate positive media contacts. Generally, the media is quite supportive of such positive programs as Habitat. Send news releases and pictures and invite coverage of first formation, groundbreaking, home blessings, etc. Media coverage will expose many persons in the local area to Habitat and confirm those already interested in the work.

When you have yourselves more or less together organizationally, it is time to think about filling out the Affiliate Application and Affiliate Covenant, which can be found in a subsequent chapter. The former requires the existence of your Board of Directors, which has begun to think through organizational goals. The latter aids in stating these goals and covenants you to basic Habitat principles.

It further commits you to the sale of decent, simple homes at no profit and no interest; a fair, non-discriminatory selection procedure; and a set of standard, simple house plans (Section III of Covenant). Both documents must be approved and signed by your board and the International Board. A project may be submitted for affiliation at either the spring or fall meetings of the International Board, at which time one of your representatives must make a presentation for approval.

Habitat for Humanity is convinced that three ingredients are essential to the success of any venture: (1) every project must have a nucleus of dedicated leaders who are willing to abandon the world's standards and to substitute the challenging "Economics of Jesus" in their dealings with His people in need; (2) there must be love in the mortar joints which holds the walls of the house together; and (3) the people must participate in working and building their community, and the houses they occupy must be (or become) their own.

SOME THOUGHTS FROM ESTABLISHED PROJECTS

1. Is there a need for decent housing in your area? Would you be able to document this need if necessary? What is the scope of other area housing organizations?
2. Find people interested in working on a Habitat project. Thoroughly introduce them to Habitat. Build your mailing list and support group. Begin your periodic newsletter.
3. General questions: Is there land or rehabitable homes available? How can they be obtained? Do you know people who might serve on the board or on committees? Are there people in need who can join in your partnership as co-workers as you begin your planning? Are there people who will help develop the program? Are there local organizations that will support you? Can you assemble a building crew of volunteers and paid workers? What sources of funding can you find? Which churches will help?
4. Consider the Board of Directors: The Board of Directors for an affiliate should represent diverse economic, religious, and ethnic groups. Lots of encouragement is a key ingredient, especially with members from the more economically disadvantaged areas. Skills to look for in prospective board members include: architect, attorney, contractor, financial expertise, knowledge of local government or other low-cost housing programs, church members, people with plenty of time and interest for the tasks in organizing a board. Aim for contributing board members. It is a good policy to have board members cover all administrative costs so that money raised for housing can be used for housing.
5. Incorporate and draw up by-laws. Excerpts from sample articles of incorporation and by-laws can be found at the end of Chapter 5. File by-laws and bank resolutions when you set up your account.
6. Apply for 501 (c)(3) tax-exempt status from the IRS. Keep your description of purpose as general as possible within the guidelines of Habitat for Humanity. Call the IRS if possible to speed up the process, but expect this to take as long as six months. Ask a nearby affiliate for a copy of their IRS application if they already have tax-exempt status. For a sample copy of this procedure, contact the Affiliate Coordinator's Office in Americus.
7. Develop your committee structure. Vital committees are fund-raising, site selection, building, and family selection. Other committees may be needed and these can be created as the need arises. Get regular reports from each committee. (A more detailed description of the four basic committees can be found in the next chapter.)
8. Find a sympathetic lawyer if one is not already on the board; one with accounting skills possibly, with a good working knowledge of the local legal process involving land titles and deeds. Your lawyer's work may be an expense item that is well worth the cost. If a competent lawyer can be found who is willing to donate

9. Constantly seek ways to spread the word about your affiliate. Start compiling a mailing list and a short periodic newsletter.
10. Set up an office and list your phone number. Decide whether or not you will rent office space or whether you will initially work out of a volunteer's home. Check with the phone company to see if you can obtain a Habitat for Humanity listing at no extra expense over a residential service cost.
11. Consider the Board of Advisors: The Board of Advisors for an affiliate should be made up of persons who can help on an "on-call" basis. The advisors may be high profile members of the community or persons with special expertise in an area, such as bankers, contractors, community workers, etc.
12. Contributed Materials and Services: All the affiliates have received contributions of various materials and labor. We have arrived at the consensus that the full value of donated materials should be charged to the job, unless the material is of greater value than what is usually used. The cost of professional labor should be charged to the job. Volunteer labor may or may not be charged, as the project deems appropriate. The concept is that the contributions are to Habitat for Humanity and not to specific families.
13. Types of Houses: Housing style depends on project site. There is a general agreement that we need to build *simple*, energy-efficient houses. Sample house plans can be ordered from the International Office at a small cost. Several of the affiliates are using passive solar designs and/or are superinsulating the homes they build.

INFLATION

Habitat does not charge interest when it sells a house. This policy is rooted in scripture (Exodus 22:25, "If you lend money to any of my people with you who is poor, you shall not... exact interest from him."), and supported by the pragmatic reality that interest prevents many poor people from having the opportunity to own a decent home. While inflation rates seem to be permanently high, Habitat believes that interest cannot be a part of its program. Some projects, like Kansas City, have shortened the length of the mortgage to 13 years in order to decrease the effects of inflation.

At first glance, it might appear that reinvestment from a non-interest Habitat mortgage would be negligible for its 20-year life due to the ravages of inflation. However, there are several aspects of the Habitat system that decrease the effects of inflation. The crucial issue for Habitat is not the general rate of inflation, or even the rate of inflation in the conventional housing market, but the increase in the cost of Habitat houses. In other words, the recycled funds are not used to buy houses on the open market but to build other Habitat houses.

While the inflation rate of the U.S. economy and its housing market has been unprecedented in the last seven years, the cost of Habitat houses has remained relatively stable due to three crucial factors: (1) volunteer labor, (2) non-interest mortgages, and (3) inexpensive land. The high cost of labor, capital, and land have pushed the average price of a house in the U.S. to $88,800. In contrast, the average Habitat house cost $24,000 in 1983, approximately the same as a Habitat house built in 1977. Inflation *does not* deplete Habitat's living endowment as rapidly as one might expect. Habitat for Humanity is proud of this surprising cost control which has counteracted the current inflationary trend in the conventional, residential real estate market.

VOLUNTEERS--AN IMPORTANT RESOURCE

Volunteers are a vital part of a Habitat for Humanity project. Volunteers, staff, and the Board of Directors are bound together by the common goal of working to provide decent housing for God's people.

At many affiliated projects, volunteers have done almost all of the work on the construction of the houses and a great deal of the office-related work. The number of dollars saved by volunteer labor is significant. Besides construction skills, there are many other skills for which volunteers may be recruited. Those who are not construction-oriented can still make important contributions to the Habitat program. For example, volunteers are needed to perform office-related work, such as personally thanking contributors for their contributions, or putting together your periodic newsletter. Other people, who are comfortable speaking before groups, can work with the fundraising and promotion committee to speak on behalf of Habitat at church programs, civic clubs, etc.

Much needs to be done in the nurturing of volunteers and in the rituals of thanksgiving when they conclude their task. Volunteers should know the importance of the work they do and should be given a great deal of reassurance and praise. Give lots of compliments early and often. Show how they have helped the mission of Habitat. Thank you notes should be sent for special efforts.

Many volunteers, with the exception of workcamps, are local. Some of the methods used to recruit volunteers are: newspaper articles and advertisements, word of mouth, time and talent sheets distributed to local churches, and sign-up sheets. Asking someone in person is best, inviting them to become partners. If you need professional help, begin by finding out if someone on the board has skills or knows someone with the skills needed who might donate their services. Then ask that person, being specific about what you want. You might want to ask the professional to be on the Board of Directors or Advisory Board of your project. Use your judgment, however, as to whether that person would be a good overall board member.

Once someone has volunteered their time, keep them active by giving them something worthwhile to do. You may want to ask them to join a specific committee. Make new volunteers feel welcome and important. If they need to learn more about Habitat, spend some time talking with them and invite them to the next showing of a Habitat slide show or film.

THE NASHVILLE AREA HABITAT'S APPROACH

The Nashville Area Habitat program used an Interest Inventory Information Sheet to survey how people would be willing to cooperate in the formation of the Nashville Area Affiliate. Organizational and committee assignments were based on this. Furthermore, Nashville Area Habitat developed a thorough, step-by-step checklist whose end point would be a strong, ongoing Habitat affiliate. These two aids are reproduced on the following four pages. Even though you may not be quite so systematic, the Nashville Area Habitat checklist is a good guide for the formation of a Habitat program. Please note that many of the items of the checklist may occur simultaneously.

NASHVILLE AREA HABITAT FOR HUMANITY: INTEREST INVENTORY INFORMATION SHEET

Name _____ Committee Interests:

Address _____ [ ] Nominating

_____ [ ] Executive

_____ [ ] Board of Directors

Telephone ( ) _____ [ ] Communication

Church Affiliation _____ [ ] Finance

_____ [ ] Fund Raising

Occupation _____ [ ] Site Selection

Specific Interests in HFH _____ [ ] Family Selection

_____ [ ] Building

_____ [ ] Others:

_____ (a) _____

_____ (b) _____

_____ (c) _____

_____   _____
(Signature)   (Date)

HABITAT FOR HUMANITY, INC.
ORGANIZATIONAL STEPS FOR ESTABLISHMENT OF A LOCAL PROJECT FROM THE NASHVILLE HABITAT FOR HUMANITY PROJECT

STATUS CODE:
Ø = In Process
0 = Completed

Status	Completion Date		Proposed Steps
		I.	Evaluation of Potential for Development of Local Project
0	_____	a.	Speak with as many people as possible on an informal basis
0	_____	b.	Have a few general meetings to discuss project and Habitat principles
0	_____	c.	Develop list of interested persons with areas of expertise
0	_____	d.	Have a guest speaker from Americus or affiliate project
0	_____	e.	Have a meeting of interested persons to decide if project is viable
		II.	Development of Basic Organizational Structure
0	_____	a.	Decide on official name for local project
0	_____	b.	Designate one person as a Registered Agent for project
0	_____	c.	Establish a headquarters for project of official address for incorporation
0	_____	d.	Prepare Articles of Incorporation
0	_____	e.	File Articles of Incorporation with Secretary of State*
0	_____	f.	File Articles of Incorporation with County Register
0	_____	g.	Prepare By-Laws (include resolutions from bank to be used)

*Prior to filing for incorporation, please submit a written request to Americus. In this request, please summarize the progress which the group has made and your plans for the immediate future. The Affiliate Office will give you a prompt written response and permission will be granted, provided the basic Habitat procedures have been followed.

Nashville HFH Organizational Steps (continued)

Status	Completion Date		Proposed Steps
0	_____	h.	Open bank account
0	_____	i.	File for Employer Identification Number
0	_____	j.	File for 501 (c)(3) tax-exempt status with the IRS
0	_____	k.	File for tax-exempt status with State
0	_____	l.	Appoint nominating committee for Board of Directors
0	_____	m.	Select Board of Directors from those nominated
0	_____	n.	Have Board elect officers and establish committee
0	_____	o.	Develop minute book for keeping accurate records
0	_____	p.	Select target area for local project house
0	_____	q.	Fill out Affiliate Application and Affiliate Covenant for HFH
0	_____	r.	Submit application for affiliation at spring or fall HFH Board meeting

III. Development of Support for Local Project

Status	Completion Date		Proposed Steps
0	_____	a.	Establish Board of Advisors to support Board of Directors
0	_____	b.	Develop brochure re: philosophy, goals, and motivation
0	_____	c.	Develop complete mailing list of concerned individuals/organizations
0	_____	d.	Send periodic newsletter to mailing list names
0	_____	e.	Send personal response to all contributions and inquiries
0	_____	f.	Send team from local project to Americus
0	_____	g.	Send couple of leaders to International Board meetings (April/October)
0	_____	h.	Speak about HFH whenever and wherever possible
0	_____	i.	Get to know people in target area ...needs, feelings, goals
0	_____	j.	Cultivate positive media contacts

IV. Commencement of Activities

Status	Completion Date		Proposed Steps
0	_____	a.	Acquire land for home construction or house for renovation

Nashville HFH Organizational Steps (continued)

Status	Completion Date		Proposed Steps
0	_____	b.	Select family for home
0	_____	c.	Raise necessary funds
0	_____	d.	Build (or renovate) home
0	_____	e.	Communicate key milestones to interested persons
0	_____	f.	Repeat steps (a) through (c) as many times as possible
0	_____	g.	Continue follow-up with appropriate committees
0	_____	h.	Continue follow-up with Board of Advisors
0	_____	i.	Continue communication through mailing list and media contacts

HABITAT RESOURCE MATERIALS

The vision of a local affiliate is fleshed out by presenting the story over and over again. The following books, audio visual aids, and promotional materials help to do that, thus providing resources for motivation to form a local Habitat.

Books

Bokotola by Millard Fuller. (1977) $4.95
    The story of the first housing project in Zaire and the events leading up to the creation of Habitat for Humanity.

Habitat Affiliate Operations Manual edited by Ted Swisher. (1985) $10.00
    Details about the ongoing questions and functions of a Habitat affiliate. (Mimeograph.)

Kingdom Building: Essays from the Grassroots of Habitat edited by David Johnson Rowe and Robert William Stevens. (1984) $4.95
    In-depth essays from the experience of Habitat partners--for leaders of local projects.

Love in the Mortar Joints by Millard Fuller and Diane Scott. (1980) $4.95
    The more complete story of Millard Fuller's personal pilgrimage and the remarkable ministry of Habitat for Humanity through 1981.

No More Shacks! by Millard Fuller. (forthcoming early 1986)
    The continuing story of Habitat for Humanity and its campaign to eliminate poverty housing.

Audio Visuals

Film (16mm):	"Shelter of God's Love" (29 min.). $25.00 rental.
Audiocassettes:	"The Economics of Jesus" (Millard Fuller), "Envisioning" (David Rowe). $3.50 each.
Slide Shows:	"Celebrate Habitat," "Celebrate Habitat Around the World," "Julia Doesn't Live Here Any More," "Love in the Mortar Joints II." $25.00 each.
Videocassettes:	"Celebrate Habitat," "Habitat Oyee," "Righteous Economics," "Shelter of God's Love," "World in Need:

Opportunity to Share." $25.00 each.

(Slide shows and videocassettes can be sent on 30-day consignment)

Other Informational Materials

"Building a Workcamp."
"Public Relations How-To Manual."
"Speakers' Resource Packet." $7.00
Miscellaneous Promotional Materials.

CHAPTER IV: BASIC COMMITTEES

The following pages contain information on how to form a Board of Directors and other basic committees you will need for a local affiliated Habitat project, along with insights and experiences gained from various affiliated projects. These committees include: the Board of Directors, Site Selection, Family Selection, Building, Fundraising (and others as needed).

As you will note, there is wide variability in how various projects have organized their committees, some establishing additional committees to the four basic ones outlined below, in accordance with the experiences they have had in fulfilling their assigned tasks. With a very small Habitat board, for instance, the same people have sometimes gravitated from committee to committee, depending upon where the action is, and a very active director and a few active board members have often found it necessary to carry the main load of the work. For the development of a better committee structure to meet the challenge of a dynamic project, responsibility and work must be broadly spread around through the use of well-functioning committees. Ideally, the committee structure will be set up with committee members appointed by the Board of Directors. Committee members should be drawn from directors, advisors, and from other actively interested individuals. If feasible, potential recipients of Habitat houses should serve on various committees.

THE BOARD OF DIRECTORS

One of the first steps to forming a Habitat affiliated project is to gather together a steering committee, committed to the vision of Habitat for Humanity in the community. At a general public meeting, individuals should be recruited to participate in the new Habitat program. In accordance with indicated interests (see Nashville's Interest Inventory, page 41), the steering committee will then organize the Board of Directors and the other basic committees. The size of the Board of Directors should conform to the laws of your state. There are many tasks included in getting a program going: publicity, public relations, administration, answering correspondence, legal matters, relations with municipal officials, and so forth. In general, the broader the ecumenical base of the Board of Directors, the more successful will be the project. A broad professional scope (lawyer, architect, construction workers, minister, administrator, businesspersons), combined with several faiths and income levels, will result in a good community representation.

A typical board is made up of officers, chosen to do specific jobs (such as president, vice-president, secretary, treasurer), and several members for a one-to-three year term. A board should be composed of people who are enthusiastic, hard-working, and committed to the goals of a Habitat project. Most of all, they must know what the job involves and they must *want* to do it. A board that is composed of members who only attend meetings does not get much done. Ideally, a candidate for the board should also be willing to serve on a committee. You need doers, so look for people who get results.

The importance of the Board of Directors cannot be overemphasized. As in any organization, a Habitat affiliate will only be as good as the people who are involved with the program. Since the limiting factor in most affiliates is a lack of funds, it makes sense to give this consideration a priority when creating a board. You don't have to invite wealthy people (although this does not hurt), but a good board needs to have some people who have business experience and financial contacts. Ministers are rarely wealthy, but they are often excellent fundraisers. Some people who have no business experience are good fundraisers, more than willing to ask for donations. Don't overlook people with this gift!

It is also wise to include people from the "community of need" on the board; Habitat's program is geared to these people and they should have substantial representation on the board. Foundations and church agencies are reluctant to contribute to an organization that does not have this type of board representation.

Homeowners should *not* serve on the board. IRS regulations state that board members of a non-profit corporation cannot benefit financially from that organization. Purchasing a Habitat house on a no-interest mortgage is definitely a benefit. Excluding homeowners from the board also prevents a tense and awkward situation should the individual fall behind on payments. (It *is* appropriate, however, for homeowners to serve on committees. Habitat wants homeowner involvement in its ministry and the board is the only place where homeowners cannot participate.)

The Board of Directors is responsible for making decisions for the affiliate as a whole. This responsibility includes: program development, fundraising, the setting of financial goals and priorities, legal matters, staff supervision, public relations, and communications with the Affiliate Coordinator's Office in Americus.

It is advisable to educate board members about Habitat. If they are not already familiar with Habitat philosophy and history, give each new board member a copy of *Love in the Mortar Joints, Kingdom Building, No More Shacks!* (and this title, the *Community Self-Help Housing Manual*). The entire board and all committee members should be familiar with Habitat's work overseas and understand how the affiliate tithe (previously discussed in Chapter II) is being put to use.

Just as the board is the key to the organization, the chairperson or president is the key to the board. The chairperson must moderate at board meetings and this is not an easy task. The ideal moderator insures that all points of view are heard and *keeps the discussion focused*. Board members love to discuss the relatively minor details of a program since most people have some familiarity with things at this level and it is easy to perceive a problem and solve it. Few people really enjoy talking about fundraising or broad policy issues because these are less clear with answers not easy to find. When the discussion evolves to the type of door knobs to be used in a house, the chairperson needs to intervene and focus the discussion.

One of the secrets of a pleasurable meeting is a sense of accomplishment. This can only happen if discussions are focused and people do their jobs in between meetings. A good chairperson does not have to be a workaholic (although lots of hard work does not hurt), but he or she should see that other people do their work. It is a good idea to contact the committee chairpersons midway between meetings and ask how their committee work is going. If the board had wanted something specific accomplished before the next meeting, remind them about it. Let them know that you would like a report for the next meeting. While the chairperson's job does not necessarily require a lot of work, it is often necessary to spend some time on the telephone, and a healthy dose of boldness is very helpful.

THE SITE SELECTION COMMITTEE

The Site Selection Committee's initial responsibility is to target the area of your community in which the ministry of Habitat will develop. Ideally, this would be done in an area in which property is readily available and can be obtained at a reasonable cost.

The committee should have three-to-five members with experience in one or more of the following areas: real estate, prior involvement in poverty housing, reside in the area (this can be a potential recipient of a house), or significant contact with those persons or agencies in a position to secure land for a Habitat project.

Once the decision to target a specific area has been made, the committee's role will be to begin the process of obtaining property for construction of the first home. Since this decision will greatly influence the method of construction to be used, it is our recommendation to integrate the Site Selection and Building Committees until the first site is selected.

The manner of acquiring property greatly varies from project to project. Habitat affiliates have often been able to obtain donated property through an individual, a corporation, or a government agency. Many property owners may be willing to contribute land or houses which they have not been able to sell. Individuals and corporations use the value of the property as a tax-deductible donation and cities or counties are often happy to get property back on the tax rolls. Habitat seldom builds in high-value real estate areas and property that may be problematic in the conventional market is ideally suited for Habitat.

In a large urban setting, open land is at a premium and what is available can be extremely expensive. Projects located in major cities, such as New York, Chicago, and Baltimore, have found that the best method of building low-cost housing is to renovate deteriorating or vacant housing. In small urban areas, land is not as difficult to acquire. For example, one affiliate was able to get the county commissioners to donate 15 acres of land at a location just outside the city limits, but well within the urban area. On the other hand, many rural projects, where land is more readily available, have been able to build cluster housing on subdivided tracts of land.

Depending on what is available or obtainable at any given time, individual projects may acquire several different types of property and use completely different methods of construction on each one. For example, in Americus many homes have been built on individual lots, other homes have been renovated on existing lots, and still others were built on a large tract of land that was subdivided for a number of homes.

By far the most widely used type of property for building a Habitat house is on a lot with ready access to utilities. While it is certainly acceptable to build on scattered sites, most projects prefer to build several houses in one area. This makes the construction work more efficient, and it also increases the visible impact that Habitat can have on a community. We believe that we can have an influence greater than the sum of the individual Habitat houses when we focus efforts in neighborhoods.

Some projects located in rural areas have obtained large tracts of land to be subdivided into individual lots. This has all the advantages of the single-lot method with one major drawback. If the tract of property does not have existing streets, sewer, or utility hook-ups, and if the local government is not willing to provide them, the cost of installing these can make the final cost of the homes beyond the reach of low-income families.

Obtaining property in an urban area normally involves a small lot and a deteriorating building. The committee should seek out sympathetic building inspectors or contractors with renovation experience to advise them before accepting this type of property. If the house is in acceptable condition, renovating is an excellent way to supply low-cost housing and revitalize deteriorating communities.

Before purchasing or accepting property, be sure to get competent legal advice and have the title searched for liens, mortgages, back taxes, right of ways, etc. The zoning laws should also be studied to make sure that the lot size is acceptable, and that you can position the desired house on the lot in the way you want it and meet the set-back requirements. It is also a good idea to check the land for drainage or moisture problems. If it is in a low area, you may be inviting serious problems that require costly solutions. If at all possible, seek the advice of a friendly, trustworthy builder or developer when purchasing property.

Occasionally, an affiliate will be offered a property that at first glance doesn't seem suitable for the project's purchase. The key to accepting such properties is creativity. The following are examples of how two affiliates have made creative use of donated properties.

The Chesapeake Habitat affiliate's first property was a donated house in very good condition, but not located in the target area. Chesapeake Habitat accepted the house with the idea of remodeling it and selling it conventionally. By making use of this property as a fundraiser, they were able to obtain $15,000 to use toward their first Habitat house.

Another affiliate, Tallahassee Habitat for Humanity, was offered several lots with deteriorated housing. Rather than letting these houses lessen the value of the properties, the project tore one down and used the salvageable materials in building new multi-family dwellings on the lots.

Seek out a person in the local tax office who is sympathetic. The tax office will have records of lots with delinquent taxes, which sometimes can be purchased from the owner in lieu of taxes owed. Tax offices also have records of city-owned property up for sale, and may be able to advise the price range to bid for a lot. (Kansas City's first bid was much too high. They were later advised of the general range and then averaged paying $667 per house-size lot.)

Check into the method used by your city to handle land and/or houses that have been acquired by the city for failure of owners to pay taxes. If your city has a land trust, there should be land or houses available which have been acquired by the city for delinquent taxes. Such property is offered for public sale, and, if there are no bidders, the property is placed in a land trust. You can then negotiate a sale from the officials who operate the trust. While Habitat does not wish to use government funds, it is both proper and desirable to acquire land or houses from whatever sources possible, including city, county, state, or federal government, as inexpensively as possible--free land is the best of all.

THE FAMILY SELECTION COMMITTEE

The Family Selection Committee should have five-to-twelve members with attributes or experience in one or more of the following areas: employment or residence in the area of need, sensitivity to poor people and their needs, a real desire to be involved in the lives of those chosen to receive houses, and enough time to visit potential recipients in their places of residence. Members of the committee must not be bashful since they will have to ask many questions of potential recipients to determine in-depth their actual need and financial situation.

It is on this committee that the integrity of your project depends. A fair, objective non-discriminatory policy, faithfully followed and widely publicized, will eliminate most criticism of favoritism. It is the Selection Committee that must wisely choose needy recipients for the houses--recipients who are too poor to get bank financing, but who are not so poor that even a no-interest, non-profit Habitat house would be a burden on their backs.

The family selection procedure needs to be flexible, yet simple. The application should include name and address of person(s) making application, family members and others living at home, place(s) of employment, income, and present housing situation. It may also include questions of how the family can contribute to the building or rehabbing of their home, why they want a home, or what type of indebtedness they presently have. Selection is based on need, ability to pay, and character.

In defining need, under no circumstances should a Habitat family be able to obtain a conventional market loan. A Habitat family is not a family that is merely priced out of the conventional market because of high interest rates. It is a family that, besides finding interest a burden, can in no way afford to pay normal bank rates; a bank would consider them a bad credit risk for a long-term home mortgage. The Habitat program is not intended to compete in the standard mortgage market or with government housing. Need also encompasses the condition of present living quarters--poor plumbing and wiring, crowded living conditions, or an unsafe structure. The number of bedrooms or the age and sex of children (especially if older boys and girls must share a bedroom) are also determinative.

Ability to pay is a rather flexible criterion in which monthly payments generally will not exceed one-fourth of the monthly income. Of course, this norm varies with size of family. The 1984 average cost of a Habitat house in the U.S. was $24,178. Over 20 years, the house payments would average a little over $100 a month.

Since it includes subjective judgment, "character" is harder to define--honesty, sincerity, the willingness to maintain a new house, and the intuitive feeling about a prospective family that is built during the personal visit and buttressed by references from others. A credit report is also a good reference check and apprises the affiliate of any serious debt problems such as judgments or possible liens; yet, a credit report should not be determinative as to whether or not a family is chosen to receive a house.

The Americus program is experimenting with a procedure which approves families on a provisional basis. Families are provisionally approved if they meet the basic criteria of need and ability to pay. They will not be fully approved unless they make a reasonable effort toward building up some sweat equity hours and paying at least a portion of their downpayment. This procedure can take a lot of the subjectivity out of the selection process. In a sense, Habitat is saying, "We think you qualify, but you need to qualify yourselves." Americus Habitat requires 500 hours of sweat equity. Homeowners receive credit for friends and relatives who come with them to work on the house. In this way, they become recruiters of volunteers just like the board. They become partners in the ministry from the beginning.

Kansas City and San Antonio Habitat utilize a one-year trial period as another way of approaching the provisional approval concept. Families rent their house for one year as Habitat gets to know them and vice versa. They may also use this time to complete sweat equity requirements. If all goes well, the rent paid becomes equity, and a deed is signed after one year. If things do not go well, the family has had a good place to live for a year at a very reasonable rent.

In some projects, a family does not qualify unless their present dwelling lacks proper plumbing, wiring, or has some severe structural problems. In other situations, overcrowding may be the reason for approval. In urban areas, a specific neighborhood may be unsuitable human habitat and households can qualify for a Habitat house on this basis. Salem County Habitat approved a family for its first house who was already living in a decent apartment. The family was approved because they took in foster children and needed more space. One of the great virtues of a non-bureaucratic organization like Habitat is that it can be free to make exceptions and be open to the unusual circumstance.

Many people wonder about families living in public housing--do they qualify for a Habitat house? There is no mandated answer. Yet, one can reason that as a Habitat house is built for a family in public housing, this allows another needy family to move into the vacant apartment. On the other hand, both Koinonia Partners and Habitat in Americus have had to deal extensively with this issue and both have decided not to build for people in public housing as a general rule. Habitat's house payments are so low that they are often equal to or lower than public housing rents. The Americus Habitat Selection Committee has been flooded with applications from public housing tenants. If families in public housing qualify, how does a committee choose the few who will receive a Habitat house? The inability to arrive at a reasonable answer to this question has led the Americus committee to decline public housing applicants.

When a family is approved, it is suggested that they open a savings account and begin saving for the downpayment, which varies among the affiliates from 1 percent to 3 percent of the cost of the house. Since following selection there is often a six-month time lag before the house is ready to be occupied, the family can begin making payments toward their downpayment to the Habitat affiliate. That the family is able and willing to sacrifice to put together a downpayment is a good indication it will be a reliable purchaser.

At a Selection Committee meeting, several dozen applications may be reviewed, with possibly less than a dozen actually selected for a home visit. If the Selection Committee is large enough, it then divides itself into groups of two who will make the home visits. At the following committee meeting, after all home visits are made, the applications are reviewed and the final selections made. Much of the selection process depends upon these home visits, which clear up any questions and make possible a thorough evaluation of present living conditions.

The purposes of the home visits are manyfold. Some are very subjective, some quite objective. The visiting committee needs to meet the applicant's family face-to-face and become better acquainted with them. The committee may also review data on the application and delve more deeply into the family situation in an open non-threatening manner. The visit should include an explanation of Habitat and its philosophy, a review of project progress, as well as the applicant's status with respect to possible selection.

A subgroup or subcommittee of the Family Selection Committee may be the most appropriate contact, naturally evolving into those persons who work with the Habitat families as concerned friends, helping them through the many changes and crises. This function, although subjective and difficult to define and depending so much upon the rapport one is able to establish, has to do with that Christian community-building that Habitat is all about.

The guidelines and sample applications that follow will aid in developing a well-functioning Family Selection Committee. Denver's family selection guidelines are broader than just selection criteria for they also deal with such topics as the mortgage, the temporary lien, Denver Habitat's first option to buy back the house, maintenance, etc. These topics are all important for the development of a good Family Selection Committee.

In an interesting letter that accompanied applications for the Beaumont affiliate's first house in Texas, the project director asked these four questions of potential applicants: (1) Is housing a very important priority for your family? (2) Do you have fairly steady work? (3) Do you have a reasonable credit record? (4) How would owning your own home make a big difference in your life?

Guidelines for the Family Selection Committee

It is the responsibility of the Family Selection Committee to screen applications, interview those who are the most likely prospects for a house, and to approve families for a purchase. Involved in this process are such details as:

1. *Making contact with the people who will be applying for a house.*
   A good place to begin is to work through existing programs in local churches, which have already made contacts in and among the low-

income population that will be served by the Habitat project. Once the process of application begins, word spreads and usually applications come freely. At the beginning, there needs to be imagination and initiative shown to make contacts with the people who will be served. As the project begins to function, it would be good to include on the Selection Committee a person who has already received a house.
2. *Explaining to applicants how the program works.* This is especially important in regard to finances. Those who are approved for a house must understand the concept of ministry behind the program. They must understand how the program is financed, especially the revolving Fund for Humanity concept. They need to be challenged to make their own contribution--no matter how small, when and if they can--by giving something over and above their monthly payment.
3. *Keeping careful records of all applications.* There must be a clear process for contacting applicants and explaining to them how their application was handled. Nothing is more frustrating for an applicant than being rejected and never informed about the decision.
4. *Preparing an application form* (see samples at end of this section). Two very basic requirements are that there be a very real need for a decent house and no other way to meet that need, and that the applicant must have the ability to make the monthly payments. Other basic criteria may be adopted by each local committee. The important thing is that the selection process be fair and simple, and that people be kept informed.
5. Commitment to the necessary time involved in committee meetings and in-home visitation for interviews with applicants.
6. Explaining to applicants the "sweat equity" portion of the program.
7. Checking with your attorney if the family has any credit problems that could become liens by the time they close on the purchase of the home.
8. Making sure that the family and/or the affiliate keep up payments on the homeowner's insurance and taxes to prevent lapse of policy or tax foreclosure.

Denver's Family Selection Criteria and Application

1. Houses will be built only for the families who do not presently have adequate housing and who do not have the financial means to build according to current conventional means.
2. Family size and need will be considered. When all other priorities are equally met, the family with the greater number of individuals will be chosen.
3. Only families with a good reputation for honesty will be selected.
4. Families chosen for homes must save and pay to Habitat a downpayment of 1 percent of the anticipated mortgage amount.

This payment must be made within six months of notification of selection, or one month prior to occupancy, whichever comes first.

5. Families are expected to assist in construction of their houses however possible. This may include clearing the lot, painting, helping with actual construction, providing food for workers, or other activities.
6. Families must demonstrate the financial resources to pay the minimum monthly payment on a regular basis. The exact payment will be determined on an individual basis.
7. A combination deed of trust/promissory note agreement will be made with the owners. The first mortgage on the property will be for the selling price of the home. A second mortgage will be placed on the property for the amount of the difference between the selling price and the appraised value. This second mortgage (and accompanying promissory note) dissolves an equal percentage each year over a five-year period for a rehabilitated home, and over a ten-year period for a new construction. The second mortgage dissolves totally at the end of the specified period.
8. Denver Habitat for Humanity will have the first option to buy back a house if the owners want to sell it. If DHFH wishes to buy it, the owner will sell it to Habitat at no more than the original cost, plus any appreciated value of the house as determined by an agreed-upon appraisal.
9. The family is responsible for maintenance and repairs of the house from the time of occupancy. The maintenance and replacement funds help encourage this. The family is also responsible for taxes and insurance, which are paid on a monthly basis in addition to house payments.
10. Lot size will meet City of Denver regulations. Houses will meet City of Denver code standards. Any additions or other buildings added to the original house are prohibited during the term of the mortgage unless approved by the Habitat board in advance.
11. Families are encouraged to contribute to the work of Habitat in a spontaneous manner. This may include money, labor, input at meetings, and so forth. When all other criteria for selection are met equally by two or more families, the one most active in the work will be chosen.
12. If more than one family meets all these guidelines on a fairly equal basis, the family who was first to submit their application shall be chosen.

DENVER HABITAT FOR HUMANITY
APPLICATION FOR A HOME

NAME_____
NOMBRE   (Head of household)
                   (Amo or ama de casa)

Address_____
Dirección

Number in family: Adults_____ Teenagers_____ Children_____
Número en la familia: Adultos   Adolescentes   Niños

Telephone_____
Teléfono

How long have you lived at your present address?_____
¿Cuánto tiempo hace que reside en esta casa?

To whom is rent paid?_____
¿A quién paga el alquiler?

How much rent do you pay?_____ per month
¿A cuánto sube el alquiler por mes?

What is your source of income?_____
¿De dónde vienen sus ingresos?

Employer_____
Empresa

Telephone_____
Teléfono

Any other sources of income?_____
¿Tiene otros ingresos?

Does anybody else in the family work?_____
¿Trabajan otros en la familia?

Where?_____
¿Dónde?

Relation_____
Parentesco

Employer_____
Empresa

DHFH APPLICATION FOR A HOME (Continued)

Telephone _____
Teléfono

In what ways can you or your family help in building or fixing your home?
¿Cómo puede usted o su familia ayudar con su casa?

_____
_____
_____

Please tell us why you want to own a home?
¿Por qué desea usted ser dueño de una casa?

_____
_____
_____

What does your family owe money on?
¿Qué clase de deudas tiene su familia?

| Item | Monthly Payment | Amount Still Left |
Deuda	Pago Mensual	Cuanto le Falta Pagar
_____	_____	_____
_____	_____	_____
_____	_____	_____

Use additional space if necessary.
Use más espacio si es necesario.

SEA ISLAND'S FAMILY SELECTION CRITERIA AND APPLICATION

SEA ISLAND HABITAT FOR HUMANITY, INC.
3363 HABITAT BLVD., JOHNS ISLAND, S.C. 29455 • (803) 768-0998

Selection Criteria for Habitat Housing

The first priority for Habitat housing is households with members who live or work or worship in the Charleston tri-county area. The applicant household must understand that an in-depth investigation will be conducted by the Selection Committee which will include personal visits and interviews by committee members.

The three (3) major areas of selection criteria are:
1. The actual need as determined by the condition of the current shelter.
2. The ability to pay for Habitat housing.
3. The character of the applicant household.

A more detailed breakdown of these three major areas of selection criteria follows:

A. Actual Need
   1. Inadequate current shelter because of problems with the heating plant, water supply, electricity, bathroom(s), kitchen, structure, etc.
   2. Inadequate number of bedrooms as determined by:
      a. Number of persons in household.
      b. Ages of household members.
      c. Sex of household members.
B. Ability to Pay for Habitat Housing
   1. No other way to meet the need for a *decent* house as determined by:
      a. Inability to secure a conventional market loan.
      b. Ineligibility for bank long-term home mortgage.
   2. "Sweat" equity, i.e., contributions of labor.
   3. Household income is not threatened by home ownership, i.e., the source of the household income stops or decreases if the applicant household owns a home.
   4. Amount of income
      a. A combined household monthly income with an approximate minimum equal to four (4) times the monthly mortgage payment and an approximate maximum equal to seven (7) times the monthly mortgage payment.

Selection Criteria for Habitat Housing (continued)

      b. Ability to pay a minimum of $600.00 as a downpayment.
C. Character Must Be Good as Determined by:
  1. Reputation for honesty.
      a. Opinions of neighbors, associated, clergy, etc.
      b. Creditors, utility companies, landlord.
  2. Cohesiveness of household unit.
      a. Husband and wife with children preferred.
      b. Relationships.
      c. Strengths.
      d. Weaknesses.
      e. Religious beliefs.
  3. Relationship to neighbors.
  4. Personal visits and interviews.
      a. Treatment of personal property.
      b. Treatment of real property.
      c. Crisis coping.
      d. "Stick-to-it-iveness."

    A point system will be used to help evaluate the applicant in each of the three (3) areas of selection criteria: need, ability to pay, and character. The point rating system will be 1 through 10, 1 being the lowest and 10 being the highest.

    Lastly, an applicant must exhibit a sincere desire for homeownership and be willing to accept the following responsibilities:
1. Disclosure of financial and personal information, e.g., places of employment, household income, marital status, present household indebtedness.
2. Follow-through on Habitat housing application requirements.
3. Contribution financially and/or otherwise to the goals of Sea Island Habitat for Humanity.
4. Assistance in the building of their Habitat house in whatever ways possible, e.g.:
    a. Cleaning.
    b. Painting and/or wallpapering.
    c. Actual renovation.
    d. Provision of food for workers.
    e. House watching.
5. Maintenance and repairs of house after occupancy.
6. Limitations of pets as per restrictive covenant.
7. Payment of property taxes and insurance, house payments, or rent.

    For an application for homeownership of Habitat housing, write to the above address or call 803/768-0998 for locations at which an application can be obtained.

SEA ISLAND HABITAT FOR HUMANITY

Application for Low-Cost Housing

DATE_____

NAME(S): (husband)_____

          SOCIAL SECURITY NO._____ AGE_____

          (wife)_____

          SOCIAL SECURITY NO._____ AGE_____

ADDRESS: _____

_____TELEPHONE NO._____

CHILDREN LIVING AT HOME (names and ages):

1._____ 4._____
2._____ 5._____
3._____ 6._____

OTHERS NOW LIVING WITH YOU (give names, ages, relationship):

1._____ 3._____
2._____ 4._____

PRESENT HOUSING SITUATION (circle appropriate words or numbers):

    Owned   Rented   Number of bedrooms 1 2 3 4

    In addition to bedrooms: kitchen   dining room
                                         bathroom   living room

    If renting, monthly rental:_____

    If applicant owns land, size of plot_____ x_____

HUSBAND'S PLACE OF EMPLOYMENT_____

    Address_____

    Length of Employment_____

    Previous Employment_____

Application for Low-Cost Housing (continued)

Reason for Leaving_____

WIFE'S PLACE OF EMPLOYMENT_____

Address_____

Length of Employment_____

Previous Employment_____

Reason for Leaving_____

FAMILY INCOME (earnings, social security, disability, welfare, etc.):

Husband's Monthly Income_____ Sources_____

_____

Wife's Monthly Income_____ Sources_____

_____

TOTAL PRESENT INDEBTEDNESS: _____

Names and Addresses of Creditors	Monthly Payment	Unpaid Balance
1.		
2.		
3.		
Totals:		

PERSONAL REFERENCES (names and addresses):

1._____
2._____
3._____

Please return this form to: SEA ISLAND HABITAT
                                      3363 Habitat Boulevard
                                      Johns Island, SC 29455
                                      Phone: 803/768-0998

THE BUILDING COMMITTEE

This committee should have three-to-seven members. They should have interest or experience in the following areas: construction work, materials acquisition, real estate, or significant contact with persons or agencies in a position to facilitate the building of the houses.

The Building Committee is responsible for the actual construction. It must coordinate labor, materials, and family interests to come up with the finished product--a decent house in a decent community for God's people in need. An important emphasis that the Building Committee ought to keep in mind is *simplicity*. One project director describes his goal as "a warm, dry house." The simpler the house, the less its costs and the more people can be served. Furthermore, people are more likely to contribute to the construction of simple but adequate houses.

Labor: The use of volunteer labor will lower your construction costs. There are areas of technical work which require skilled licensed contractors, but on any house there is much that can be done by volunteers. The main requirements with volunteers is that there be a responsible, preferably skilled, person in charge.

Most projects are small enough to cover administrative input through volunteer labor. Some also combine supervised volunteer labor with hired contractors, while others subcontract all work. Sometimes sympathetic contractors or union locals will donate their labor toward the project. The International Office's construction crew in Americus is all-volunteer labor. Lee County Habitat and other affiliates have had retired builders donate time to supervise the construction of the houses.

Box Elder, Utah; Omaha, Nebraska; and other affiliates have used vocational education students to complete work on their houses. The Omaha affiliate appreciated the work the students did, but experienced strong financial pressure in keeping to the school system's schedule, rather than Habitat's schedule.

Materials and Methods: Meeting local building codes is necessary and can sometimes be difficult. Working with a local contractor is a great help in dealing with local codes.* As costs of materials are constantly rising, use your imagination to secure materials. In San Antonio, a contractor working primarily in the remodeling field has donated materials to Habitat. Houses which are to be demolished are

---

*Two good sources on nationwide codes are: *One and Two Family Dwelling Code* (International Conference Building Office, 5360 S. Workman Mill Road, Whittier, CA 90601, $12.00), and Edmund Vitale's *Building Regulations: A Self-Help Guide for the Owner-Builder* (Charles Scribner's Sons, 597 Fifth Avenue, New York, NY 10017, $4.95).

good sources of usuable materials. An old house may even be purchased, torn down, and materials used for a new house. Immokalee bought six houses which had been condemned for demolition and dismantled them for materials. Be experimental with materials for your area. Explore the use of logs, pole construction, and earth (berm) construction to keep materials costs low and energy savings high. Some contractors and materials supply outlets have even donated refurbishings to the projects, especially paint, tile, and carpeting. Further, a solar designer or a modular home manufacturer may be willing to donate some, if not all, of the materials for a house if the house could be used as a model home for a month or two.

Energy Efficiency: One crucial consideration for almost all parts of the continental U.S. and Canada is energy efficiency. An energy-inefficient house, even if it is cheaper to build, will prove to be no bargain for low-income persons who can't afford soaring electric or heating bills. It is not necessary to go in for "exotic" active solar heating devices, such as hot water heaters with rooftop collectors (although a number of low-cost ones with reasonable operating efficiencies are now available). Much can be accomplished through design and proper siting of the house.

Adequate cross-ventilation is a must for cooling efficiency; overhangs on south-facing windows are another plus. Using such earth materials as rock, adobe, or rammed earth blocks increases the insulation effect and lowers insurance rates. Thermal Belt Habitat in Tryon, North Carolina uses a "solar attic" to move hot air out in summer and a heated slab to retain warm air in winter. In colder areas, such common-sense techniques of passive solar heating as the proper siting of a house (ordinarily on an east-west axis), window placement (most on the south, least on the north), and *sufficient* insulation are crucial to energy efficiency. Look also into super-insulation, such as the Larsen Truss system for the owner-builder or renovator.

The point about insulation is especially important because it will increase costs. But these costs are only a fraction of the total and will repay themselves many times over in reduced heating bills. Furthermore, installation of adequate insulation is easy when the house is being constructed, but much harder and more expensive after it is built. If a basement is planned, be sure that it is insulated below the frost line. (The best technique in very cold climates is to take insulation, such as styrofoam, even below the slab in the basement floor. That means making a decision on insulation *before* the foundation is completed.)

Saving Electricity: In all regions of North America but especially those with high electric rates, reducing electricity consumption is as good as providing a continuing subsidy to a low-income family. Important advances in recent years make it possible to cut electricity use to a mere fraction of what it once was (and still is, in most houses).

Amory Lovins, founder of the Rocky Mountain Institute and

author of *Soft Energy Paths,* has been one of the pioneers in the effort to reduce electricity consumption by increasing efficiency. The Intermediate Technology Development Group of North America is now exploring with him appropriate ways of sharing the fruits of his work with those involved in creating or improving housing for low-income people. Write to Save Electricity, ITDG/NA, Suite 9A, 777 United Nations Plaza, New York, NY 10017 for further information.

Mode of Operation: The Building Committee will discuss with the prospective family their preferences on such matters as the number of bedrooms, basic floor plan, and the arrangement of the house, especially the kitchen. Various floor plan booklets are available, including the "Economy Homes" booklet published by the Standard Homes Plan Service in Fuquay-Varina, North Carolina. A collection of other plans can be ordered from the International Office of Habitat in Americus, Georgia. (See the Appendices for details on both of these.) Sample house plans and a bibliography of sources on low-cost, energy efficient housing can also be found at the end of this *Manual.*

The Americus office has developed some house plans for affiliated projects with four-bedroom houses at 1,050 to 1,150 square feet. This will meet the needs of a large family. A typical three-bedroom Habitat house is 900 to 1,000 square feet. Again, while not spacious it is sufficient. Even though some families can afford a larger house at no interest, we must realize that our resources are limited and an extra 100 square feet for one family is a bedroom less for another family. Habitat can build an entire house in Haiti for the cost of an extra bedroom in the United States.

Simplicity in design and construction techniques are essential also if much of the construction is to involve the "sweat equity" of the homeowner through his or her own labor. However, very substantial savings can be achieved even if the homeowner is willing or able only to handle interior and exterior finishing, including landscaping. Depending on the time and skills of the homeowner (and what local building codes will allow), these can range from simply painting (inside and out) to interior partitioning, sheetrock (or other interior wall-covering) installation, plastering, tiling or carpeting floors, and installing molding.

Where skills and time are substantial, the house can be sold as a shell, letting the homeowner do (or arrange for) his or her own plumbing and electrical work (again depending on local codes) and insulation, as well as interior partitioning. Another approach to cutting the initial cost is to have only the most essential rooms finished (completely or only roughly), letting the homeowner do the rest after occupancy.

Particular attention should be paid to the two following points. Small pre-formed bath units may make it possible to have two baths which can be very useful to a large family and may cost no more than one large bath. Keep hall space to a minimum; halls consume energy but are necessary to insure more privacy and easier access to bedrooms.

Rehabilitation: Many interested persons have asked whether Habitat is involved in rehabilitation, as well as in new house construction. The answer is "Yes." A significant amount of work is now beginning to go into rehabilitation. If a given building is structurally sound, you may add many year's life to that building at a considerably lower investment than would be required for a new building. There are ways of locating houses that can be rehabilitated: by contract with present owner-occupiers, possibly through an urban homesteading program, or through a "bargain sale," tax-deductible method. The latter two programs, of course, must be thoroughly reviewed legally. It goes without saying that a Habitat program does not rehabilitate renter-occupied buildings. That would defeat one of the purposes of Habitat--that of empowering the poor through home ownership.

A number of affiliates, notably the Appalachia Habitat (headquartered in Robbins, Tennessee), operate rehabilitation/repair programs to complement their homebuilding program. A rehabilitation program may even precede a homebuilding program, giving the affiliate Board of Directors a sense of progress, while acquainting the community with the concepts behind Habitat. This was the case for Western North Carolina Habitat (Asheville), which continues with both programs.

THE FUNDRAISING COMMITTEE

Your Fundraising Committee is enormously important since without money, you will build no houses. The committee should have at least a dozen members, but even more is preferable. Furthermore, everyone must be involved in fundraising; members should be enthusiastic about Habitat for Humanity and anxious to share the story with anyone who will listen. Experience in fundraising is helpful but not essential. Enthusiasm and determination are indispensable.

The Fundraising Committee is very critical to your overall program. Even housing for low-income families is very capital-intensive. In the presentation for your Affiliate Application you need to think through your goals, and how you plan to go about raising funds to meet those goals. Fundraising does not require any new or unusual skills. It does require calls and letters to groups and individuals, personal visits, and follow-up calls and letters. Persistence is the key. If one door closes, proceed to another and another.

Individuals, Church, and Foundation Involvement: The person(s) involved in your fundraising ought to be good in public relations and actually enjoy it. Seek out an active, dynamic go-getter as chairperson of the Fundraising Committee, and under his/her direction start knocking on many doors. A more academic type may be preferred for writing foundation proposals. A mix of fundraising approaches is beneficial. One local project persuaded a college president in the area to serve as honorary chairman of their fundraising drive. A respected banker, if you have the support of his/her bank, may also be a good chairperson.

Your fundraising team needs to go to church groups, mission societies, human needs committees, Sunday School classes, and even main Sunday morning worship services. Yet, the purpose of fundraising is not to hardsell Habitat. While definitely a part of the broader Christian mission, Habitat is only one example of Christian mission--but, we believe, a good one.

Persons who present your local program should be very familiar with the local affiliate's goals and well versed in Habitat philosophy as a specific example of mission--in the inner city, as well as overseas activity. *Love in the Mortar Joints, Bokotala,* and *Kingdom Building* are very good aids. Let these materials buttress your own convictions. In the presentation, seek to inspire as well as inform people. Challenge people to become involved locally or internationally, wherever their interests lie. Habitat is an idea whose time has come, and people are ready to join forces. When presentations are made, encourage people to read the above books, leave handout materials, obtain additions to your local mailing list, and challenge people to become physically and financially involved. Some may observe, "Your efforts are so little." Remind them that the 1,000-mile journey begins with one step. We must work with what we have, even in small ways. Whatever you say, compliment others' efforts; do not downgrade them.

At first, presentations will be based on the track record of Habitat for Humanity International and other established affiliates. Use Habitat's "Love in the Mortar Joints" slide show or film "Shelter of God's Love" with any addition of your own, perhaps later developing your own full-scale presentation. As soon as possible, you should develop your own brochure and begin at least a quarterly newsletter (an important mechanism for maintaining interest) and write a basic project statement which concisely presents goals, philosophy, and dreams. Wherever you are, have materials to put into people's hands, so that they can take something home with them. Every time you speak, and in every way you can, start developing a local mailing list.

Since Habitat's basic philosophy is Christian, fundraising naturally is closely associated with churches. Use every method of contacting local churches and/or church-related groups in your area. Explain Habitat to them and seek their financial support. Most project money comes from individuals and church groups.

If you know of a foundation (church-related or secular) that makes grants for such projects as housing, contact them. Find out if the foundation is compatible with Habitat in philosophy and operation. If so, make a formal appeal for a grant, making certain that all of the necessary information is sent. Then keep in touch. It may take a long time to process your application, so keep the foundation informed of your progress as you wait. Check with the Chamber of Commerce or local library regarding the existence of such foundations. Write the

Affiliate Coordinator of Habitat International for general information on how to approach foundations.

In fundraising, be prepared to answer the following questions:

1. Exactly what is the purpose of your project?
2. What proof do you have that you will provide a real service?
3. How do you compare with existing programs of this type? Do you work with other local housing programs?
4. Will you expand your work in the future (financial as well as building goals)?
5. How do people qualify for your program's services?
6. What is your total operating budget?
7. What is your cost of serving each person who comes to you?
8. What is the relationship of your staff size to the number of people served?
9. How recent are the figures you have quoted?
10. Where are you located in town?

Cultivate volunteer fundraisers: motivate and train them. Once you find a contributor, keep him or her informed of your work so that they will be more likely to continue their support.

Use Habitat materials for brief introductory programs in churches and other places where people gather; they are well-conceived and demonstrate a track record. The Habitat slide show is a good way to make an introductory approach to a class, civic group, or study group. Contact people who have connections with groups, those who might arrange some Habitat presentations.

A second avenue of fundraising (often not thought of as fundraising for a project such as Habitat) are no-interest loans. Many persons do not feel financially secure enough to make an outright project donation, yet can make a no-interest loan. Thus, funds can be immediately available to push construction along. Repayment of no-interest loans is generally made on the basis of a 30-day notification period. The *Habitat Affiliate Operations Manual* has sample guidelines for no-interest loans. If you accept loans above $10,000 from one individual, there may be problems with imputed interest. The law currently is unclear on this matter. Consult a local tax lawyer or contact the Americus office for the latest information on this subject.

In any case, what is really instrumental in fundraising is a person convinced that what he or she is espousing is an idea whose time has come. What Habitat is and what Habitat is about needs to be communicated enthusiastically before people involve themselves in such a project.

Habitat efforts have always been grassroots efforts. Through individual and church contacts, people, Sunday School classes, and congregations are challenged to give as much as they can, and to become involved in any way they can. Habitat's approach is that of consciousness-raising; sowing the seeds of the challenge of the Habitat vision--non-profit, no-interest mortgages for God's people in need--and of the meaningful involvement that this entails. Clarence Jordan,

Habitat's spiritual father, used to say that we must become "monumental beggars" for Christ.

The overwhelming way Habitat has done this is through speaking engagements, slide presentations, and "mission" programs (which are key forums). The media--TV, radio, and newspapers are interested in Habitat and give local credibility. Personally acknowledge all gifts with a "thank you" letter for that builds a two-way relationship, as does a periodic newsletter. Employment of volunteers and workcamps (once construction has begun) also spread the word.

Besides the above direct approaches, there are other activities that have involved many people and raised funds to meet project needs. These include paper drives, aluminum can collections, garage sales, car washes, "slave" days, etc. Walk-a-thons, racquetball-a-thons, bike-a-thons, rocking chair-a-thons, bowl-a-thons, and the like have also been quite successful, and have often involved new people. Book sales and Sunday School projects, including challenges and "matching" gifts, are also good. Challenging people to tithe their mortgage payments is a novel, yet meaningful, approach.

All the above are grassroots approaches. That has been the historical strength of Habitat. Use your creativity to "flesh out" these ideas with your real-life situations. The *Habitat Affiliate Operations Manual* has other ideas and aids, but the key ingredient is each project's local initiative using these time-proven methods. They do require a lot of work, but they also build a local Habitat project.

OTHER COMMITTEES

While the above four committees are essential to every Habitat affiliate, some projects have discovered the need to develop other committees as they grow. Garrett County Habitat not only has a Fundraising Committee, but also Publicity and Finance Committees, and has added Volunteer and Workcamp Committees as well. Chesapeake Habitat formed its Volunteer Committee very early on.

The Volunteer Committee is responsible for developing and implementing a plan to identify, recruit, orient, and schedule volunteers to assist with office administration, construction, and collecting donated material. It works closely with the Building Committee to insure that contracted paid laborers are not deterred by volunteer labor, as well as to insure that volunteers have appropriate job assignments. Not only does the Volunteer Committee coordinate volunteer labor (and workcamps) but it actively solicits them.

The Volunteer Committee establishes a file or master file of interested volunteers, identifying their particular skills. Through coordination with the construction supervisor, volunteers are contacted at the appropriate time. Garrett County Habitat wrote in their 1984 Annual Report, "Because of the difficulty in anticipating the progress of work done through volunteers, the scheduling was not easy. It was stressful at times and required a belief that God would provide. God did!"

Board members, staff, and volunteers should work as a team, even if they are inclined to do it alone. The strongest and most durable projects are remarkable for how much the work is shared. Especially at Habitat affiliated projects without paid staff, it is essential to share leadership in order to cover the times when illness, transfers, or travel will deplete the leadership. The more people involved, the broader your base will be and the harder it will be to collapse under the strain. The single most common problem in a volunteer organization is "burn out," but "an ounce of prevention is worth a pound of cure." The more volunteers recruited, the less chance that two or three people will be doing all the work. Remember that the board is responsible for the growth, integrity, and health of yourselves, the Habitat affiliated project, and the volunteers. Keep your sense of humor! Humor keeps everything in perspective and keeps you going. Plan some fun and enjoy Habitat celebrations as often as possible.

Volunteers that work with an affiliated project for an extended period of time need to have housing and a subsistance allowance if they do not have any other means of support. In Americus, volunteers receive free housing and utilities. A stipend of $20 per week is given to each volunteer with an additional $25 subsidy per month. The volunteer is expected to work five days a week from 8:00 a.m. to 5:00 p.m. Projects that cannot operate during normal weekday hours find that a regular schedule on evenings and weekends avoids the problem of notifying workers about last-minute changes. For example, a schedule of Tuesday and Thursday evenings and all-day Saturday provides opportunities for people who cannot work at other times.

A few projects, such as Garrett County Habitat mentioned above, have decided to subdivide the Fundraising Committee, separating out the functions of promotion and public relations from the broader fundraising function. Habitat is a very newsworthy effort. Television news editors, newspaper editors, religious and civic leaders, are generally quite receptive to Habitat-type public interest stories. Pastors, lay leaders, and mission committee chairpersons are also very open to learning about Habitat. Such contacts must be cultivated through personal relationships, and often by the writings of press releases and stories. Also, after personal contacts have been made, they should be kept informed about what is happening in Habitat (locally, nationally, internationally) through the local and national newsletters. Don't forget to put these contacts on the Habitat mailing lists.

Given the volume of this work, a subcommittee or even a separate committee may be set up in charge of promotion and public relations. It will coordinate presentations to churches, civic clubs, and the media, as well as be in charge of literature, books, publicity, etc. An advantage of subdividing the Fundraising Committee is that finance and public relations often involve two different types of people with two different sets of problems. The finance people may be interested in accounting for or investing funds. The public relations people are concerned with promoting an image which will help raise funds for the affiliate.

The Omaha affiliate utilizes *ad hoc* or special committees to draw in non-members to work on specific projects. These committees may plan a benefit dinner, may conduct workshops for the affiliate, or coordinate a summer workshop. They are dissolved after their project goal is reached.

CHAPTER V: ORGANIZATIONAL REQUIREMENTS

BECOMING AN AFFILIATE

Affiliated projects are those projects organized according to the purpose and philosophy of Habitat for Humanity, but for which Habitat is not primarily responsible in providing funds, personnel, or program development. Habitat will help with these tasks to the extent possible. Affiliated projects, morally and spiritually, covenant to improve inadequate housing in their local areas.

The Affiliate Covenant defines the purposes and philosophy of Habitat for Humanity to which an affiliate agrees when it joins Habitat for Humanity, Inc. The Covenant is the moral and spiritual document signed by a given affiliate and is tied to other affiliated projects, to the Affiliate Council, to the International Board, and to the sponsored projects.

Both the Affiliate Application and Affiliate Covenant must be approved and signed by your board and the International Board. A project may be submitted for affiliation at either the spring or fall International Board meetings, at which time one of your representatives must make a presentation in favor of your approval to the International Board. The Covenant is the document that both Habitat International and the local Habitat affiliate agree to follow as part of their mutual commitment.

Habitat International has no required selection criteria or house plans other than the general commitments made in the Covenant. It is covenanted that selection criteria be fair and non-discriminatory, and house plans be simple. You will have to struggle with the various Covenant agreements, but in the end, they will be yours. Thus is the autonomy of the local decision making maintained and, in fact, reinforced. Simplicity of house design is absolutely necessary if costs are to be kept low. Changes to the original house design that increase its cost must be paid for by the new homeowner "up front" before installation. This policy is set so as to avoid the gradual chipping away of funds out of the Fund for Humanity for luxury items.

In summary, the Affiliate Application process is as follows. Following the general direction of the *Community Self-Help Housing*

Manual, a local committee organizes itself into a Board of Directors, formulates its goals, and draws up its Articles of Incorporation and By-Laws. During this time, Habitat for Humanity, Inc. may appoint a "guide" who would be available to answer questions and give advice when needed, usually through the Affiliate Coordinator's office. The Affiliate Application and signed Affiliate Covenant must be submitted to Americus by March 15 if the Affiliate Application is to be considered at the April International Board meeting, or by September 15 if the Application is to be considered at the October meeting. Additionally, representatives from a proposed project *must* attend the entire board meeting at which they present their Affiliate Application for review and approval. It is expected that all affiliates will have at least one representative at the annual International Board meeting each October.

If approved, it is through the Affiliate Council that a new affiliated program will relate to other affiliated programs and to the International Board of Directors. The Affiliate Council serves as a clearinghouse for promotional and technical information and for the interchange of volunteers. It was at the October 1982 International Board meeting that the Affiliate Council was created by Habitat's Board of Directors at the suggestion of affiliate project leaders. The Affiliate Council is composed of all the affiliated projects. Representation on the Council is automatic with application and approval of an affiliated project as a member of the Habitat family. Each affiliated project has one vote in any decision made by the Affiliate Council. Subsequently, the Affiliate Coordinator was employed as a permanent member of the Americus staff to implement the purposes of the Affiliate Council. As such, the Affiliate Coordinator serves as the liaison among the affiliated programs, and as the staff contact between the affiliates, the Americus staff, and the International Board of Directors.

The first major purpose of the Affiliate Council is to serve as a clearinghouse for technical, promotional, and fundraising information that will benefit the affiliates. An outgoing Watts line and operations bulletins are instruments which facilitate these processes. Other materials are periodically available from the Americus office.

Included at the end of this chapter is the Affiliate Covenant and the completed Affiliate Application from the Tupelo, Mississippi project. They show the thought and planning that goes into the Affiliate Application. The Affiliate Coordinator maintains personal contact with the affiliates so as to aid and strengthen each affiliate as much as possible. Furthermore, in conjunction with the Director of Volunteer Services, volunteers and workcamps are directed to the affiliates as the affiliates are able to meaningfully employ and accommodate them.

LEGAL INCORPORATION

You may decide to launch your Habitat project under the umbrella of an existing non-profit organization whose programs are consistent with the purpose of Habitat for Humanity, Inc. Several local projects have been started this way and such a procedure is quite acceptable. However, sooner or later, your group will need to form its own non-profit corporation.

The first step in forming your own non-profit corporation is to secure the services of a good lawyer--possibly even a retired lawyer. Perhaps you will have one within your group who will donate his services. If not, it is better to pay for competent legal services than to cajole a lawyer into doing the work when his heart is really not in it and then waiting months to receive free services.

You must decide on the official name of your group. To affiliate with Habitat for Humanity, Inc., the words "Habitat for Humanity" must be part of your name. The name should be descriptive of the area you expect to serve, such as Beaumont Habitat for Humanity, Garrett County Habitat, and so forth. Avoid using a name that is too vague or encompasses a large geographic region unless you can realistically serve that area. In general, it is best to name your project after the city or county you will serve. As a first step, your lawyer will apply to the Secretary of State of your state to reserve the exclusive right to use the corporate name you have chosen.

Next, the Articles of Incorporation and By-Laws must be prepared to conform to the laws of your state. The purpose should be exactly, or at least essentially, those of Habitat for Humanity. (See the excerpts from the Articles of Incorporation and the Preamble from the By-Laws later in this chapter.) The Affiliate Coordinator's office can supply you with a sample copy of incorporation documents, possibly from your state, which can be compiled almost verbatim by your lawyer, since the language pertains to aspects of your non-profit corporation that are essential to be declared tax-exempt 501 (c)(3)-- that is, a non-profit corporation that can receive tax-deductible contributions from individuals. (See the following section on tax-exempt status.) Where and how to file your Articles of Incorporation varies from state to state. Your lawyer will know how to do this and advise what the costs will be, usually quite nominal. You can also save your lawyer time by checking a legal form book for your state at a local law library which will contain language particular to your state.

TAX-EXEMPT STATUS

As soon as you are incorporated, you should apply for tax-exempt status with the Internal Revenue Service. You should write a letter to your district director of the IRS and request Publication 557, "How to Apply for Recognition of Exemption for an Organization," and Package 1023, "Application for Recognition of Exemption." In your letter, state that you have formed a 501 (c)(3) non-profit corporation and you wish to apply for tax-exempt status. You must apply for tax-exempt status within 15 months of your date of incorporation.

When you receive the requested materials, read them carefully, fill out the required forms completely, and ask your lawyer to review them. This will greatly expedite approval of your application. You should get an advance ruling on your application within three to six months (but don't be surprised if it takes even longer). The Americus office can send you a copy of a successfully submitted application of another affiliate if this would be helpful.

Each year in the future, you will be required to file a form 990 with the IRS. It is important to remember to do this. There is a fine for not doing so. Instructions are given in the materials you will receive from the IRS.

After you have received your advance ruling letter declaring you a tax-exempt organization by the IRS, you should file to be declared a tax-exempt organization by your state. You can get the necessary forms by writing to the appropriate state agency in your state capitol. In Georgia, non-profit organizations must file form 3105, "Application for Recognition of Exemption" under Georgia Code Section 92-3105. This form must be sent to the Office of Attorney General and to the State Revenue Commissioner, Trust and Estate Section in Atlanta, along with copies of Articles of Incorporation, By-Laws, and letters from the IRS granting tax-exempt status. The exact procedure to be followed in your state may be different, but something similar to the above will be required.

Your state will probably require you to file an annual report with the appropriate state agency. In Georgia, all tax-exempt organizations must file annually with the state a copy of the forms they file with the IRS (form 990). You should also check to see if your affiliate may be exempt from sales tax for the materials it purchases.

DOCUMENTS NEEDED WHEN YOU SELL A HOUSE

As with previous matters in this chapter, you will need the services of a lawyer when you select your first family and are ready to begin preparing the several necessary legal documents agreed to in the deed and to provide for eventual transfer of ownership to the family. The *Habitat Affiliate Operations Manual* will also help here as it goes into considerable detail on what other projects have done.

The basic documents used to sell a house on mortgage vary from state to state. In Georgia, these are the Real Estate Sales Contract, the Warranty Deed, the Deed to Secure Debt, the Promissory Note, and the Settlement Statement. Each state has standard legal forms for all the documents you will ordinarily need to sell a house. You will need to "tailor" these to conform to the particular characteristics of your program, but in all cases remember that, as much as possible, Habitat seeks to follow the free market model. The standard legal forms are generally available in a commercial stationary store, which also serves a number of law offices. When you get stuck, seek help from a lawyer friend. Standard legal forms are widely used for routine purposes, such as residential real estate transactions, and any lawyer engaged in general law practice will be able to help you.

All Habitat projects encourage families to do volunteer work on their own house as well as others in the project. In Immokalee, Omaha, Chicago, and other affiliates, such "self-help" work is mandatory. Guidelines should be formulated on procedures.

At every stage in your dealings with the family that will receive the new house, beginning with the very first time you meet them, share the philosophy of Habitat and the Christian motivation of the work. Make certain that they understand that you are there to share with them in more ways than just receiving a house, and that they can contribute to the work, as others have done, to make their house a reality. Tell them about your local newsletter and the newsletter from the International Office, and add them to both mailing lists to be kept informed about the ongoing work in your area and in other places. Explain how every house payment they make will be "recycled" to build houses for other people in need, as with those before them. Make sure that they understand the importance of making their payments regularly, and even accelerating payments if their economic situation improves.

A special "house dedication" is encouraged after the house is completed and the family has moved in. The deeds can be signed and presented at this time, or later, if preferred. Family members and friends can be invited to the occasion, and if the new owners are active in a local church, the minister and other church members should be included. Once more, use this opportunity to explain the philosophy of Habitat and its unique method of using capital by recycling payments, inviting those present to help others as others have helped this family.

DELINQUENT PAYMENTS

No one wants to have to follow up on delinquent payments. However, just as sure as night follows day, there will be situations where monthly payments are delinquent. In most standard mortgages, foreclosure proceedings can start if payments are 30 days in arrears. Habitat does not operate in the same way as a conventional lender: proceedings are more long-suffering than in the private market. Yet, for the integrity of Habitat and for the integrity of what is said to donors, as well as for the dignity fostered through homeownership, there must be teeth in each project's policy regarding delinquent mortgage payments.

First in consideration must be the facts of the situation.

Delinquent payment and foreclosure policy ought not be so mechanical as to ignore personal hardship. For example, there is a definite difference between a situation where a family is behind in its house payments merely because it does not or cannot manage funds, and where a family is temporarily suffering from financial hardship. In both cases, counseling is appropriate by someone related to Habitat, sensitive to the situation, and able to establish rapport with the family.

The Appalachia Habitat delinquent payment policy was adopted by its Board of Directors in October 1979, but never forced to be fully implemented. One unemployed resident, delinquent in payments, was able to work off his back payments by doing a necessary job for Appalachia Habitat itself.

Appalachia philosophy on delinquent payments is to get the family to deal with the problem and make an effort toward payment. First month (30 days delinquent)---grace period, with notice sent that payment was missed. Second month (60 days without payment)---an official visit will be made to the family's home by a Habitat representative to determine why payments have been missed and to work out a payment schedule. The visit will be written up. Third month (90 days without a payment)---a notice of foreclosure will be sent to a lawyer who will send a letter to the family announcing foreclosure unless payment is made. A penalty of $50 will be assessed to the family's payments to be sent to the attorney. Fourth month (120 days without payment)---GONE. If no attempt at payment is made, Habitat will foreclose after 120 days.

It is encouraging to note that from the hundreds of homes built, there have been very few foreclosures. When a family has a good home for the very first time in their lives, they want to hold on to it. Furthermore, they are aware of the fact that their payments help others as they have been helped. It is very effective to take a family "next in line" to visit the delinquent family so that they can be reminded that their funds are needed.

A BASIC COVENANT BETWEEN HABITAT FOR HUMANITY, INC., AND AN APPROVED AFFILIATED PROJECT

Preface

Habitat for Humanity, Inc. and the Habitat Affiliate work as partners to spread the Habitat vision. Although Americus will assist all it can, especially in the coordination of expertise, project publicity, and solicitation of funds, it is the Affiliate which is directly responsible for organization, fundraising, construction, and legal affairs.

I. The Purpose of Habitat for Humanity

Through loving acts and spoken word, our desire is to exalt Jesus Christ as Lord.

In its Habitat program globally, Habitat for Humanity seeks to give witness to the Christian gospel by working in partnership with God's people in need to create a decent habitat in which to live and work. The aim is to create an environment of hope, dignity, and a truly human existence for all people; as much as possible, this should be done with the recipients of houses making the decisions regarding their development.

Wherever possible, we would cooperate with other agencies that have similar purpose, and we seek an ever-expanding company of persons to participate in this ministry.

II. Basic Assumptions that Undergird the Work of HFH

1. Because we have been loved and cared for in God's provision, we wish to share that love and goodness with brothers and sisters in need anywhere, within the bounds of our resources.
2. That Habitat for Humanity is a people-to-people partnership ministry aimed at the development of persons, not merely the construction of houses.
3. The overall project operation will be without profit and without interest and free of government control. Government funds will not be used to build Habitat houses. It is a people-to-people project of love under the lordship of Jesus Christ. However, streets, utilities, land, or old houses needing rehabilitation, may be acquired from government agencies if no strings are attached that violate Habitat principles. That assumes that the Habitat concept is justifiable grounds for appeals for a stewardship response from Christians anywhere.

4. The Habitat program will proceed on an ecumenical basis.
5. All income from repayment of loans will be used for the work of the Fund for Humanity.
6. Preferential treatment, bribes, or sub-renting of houses by owners as a profit-making matter is contrary to Habitat philosophy.
7. That there will be developed a process providing a flow of information that would be mutually beneficial and encourage true dialogue.

III. Assumptions which Undergird the Affiliate Relationship

1. That Habitat's services are offered in response to mutually agreed-upon requests from the administering Affiliate of any community.
2. That there is a locally autonomous leadership which shares Habitat's philosophy and with which Habitat can consult.
3. That there is the formation of a structure to help facilitate a mutually caring community served by the Habitat Affiliate in which participants respond spiritually, socially, and monetarily to the needs of their neighbors.
4. That when a specific project is completed and paid for, participants will be encouraged to continue to contribute to the Fund for Humanity in order to help create other projects, possibly in nearby communities.
5. That Habitat for Humanity, Inc. will provide minutes of its board meetings to each Habitat Affiliate, which in turn will forward the requested reports to the Americus office.

IV. Requirements for Affiliations with Habitat for Humanity, Inc.

1. All houses shall be sold with no profit added and no interest charged.
2. Pre-determined criteria for the fair and non-discriminatory selection of families to receive houses, and of a plan of publicity for soliciting applications will be prepared.
3. A list of the expectations of participation by each family to receive a house, such as contractual agreements, down payments, progress payments, "sweat equity," community responsibility, etc.
4. That each Affiliate commit itself to develop ties with the total Christian community in its area.
5. All Habitat finances and assets be kept separate, strictly accounted for, and used strictly in accordance with Habitat purposes.
6. A projected statement of sources of income and a specific fund-raising plan for the first and second years of the project is required.
7. That the local committee shall organize in accordance with local laws so as to be a non-profit organization, contributions to which will be tax deductible.

8. Basic house plans will reflect the Habitat philosophy of building simple but adequate houses. Changes or additions beyond the basic house plan will be the sole responsibility of the owner who will assume those costs.
9. Each Affiliate is expected to send at least one representative to Habitat's annual (fall) meeting.

ANNUAL REPORTS

(Overview: Reports result in a better organized project. Shared reports keep partners informed.)

1. A financial report, including an income and expense statement and balance sheet.
2. A list of board members: names, addresses, religious affiliation, and their project-related activity.
3. An estimate of the total number of people now occupying Habitat houses.
4. A general inspection of houses and grounds--maintenance and appearance.
5. A general statement on status of house payments and on what is being done if any are in arrears.
6. Cost breakdown on a typical average-sized house completed during the previous year.
7. Statement on construction status--each house, with percent completed.
8. Future construction plans.
9. Statement on use of workcamps.
10. Additional comments and concerns.
    (These Annual Reports are to come out as a questionnaire from the Director of Operation's office at the beginning of December.)

An on-site evaluation will be made for each project every two years and will include a confirmation of the information submitted above. The evaluation will be done by one staff person and one Advisor or Director if possible.

With the purpose and assumptions of Habitat for Humanity being understood by both parties, and having agreed to the conditions herein set forth, we hereby commit ourselves to work together toward the completion of the _____
affiliated Habitat project.

This covenant must be approved by a majority of the Habitat Board of Directors, as well as the Affiliated Committee.

Date _____
                    (For the _____Habitat Affiliate)

                    (For Habitat Board of Directors)

SAMPLE COMPLETED AFFILIATE APPLICATION
OF
NORTHEAST MISSISSIPPI HABITAT FOR HUMANITY

APPLICATION FOR AFFILIATION
Habitat for Humanity, Inc.
419 West Church Street
Americus, GA 31790

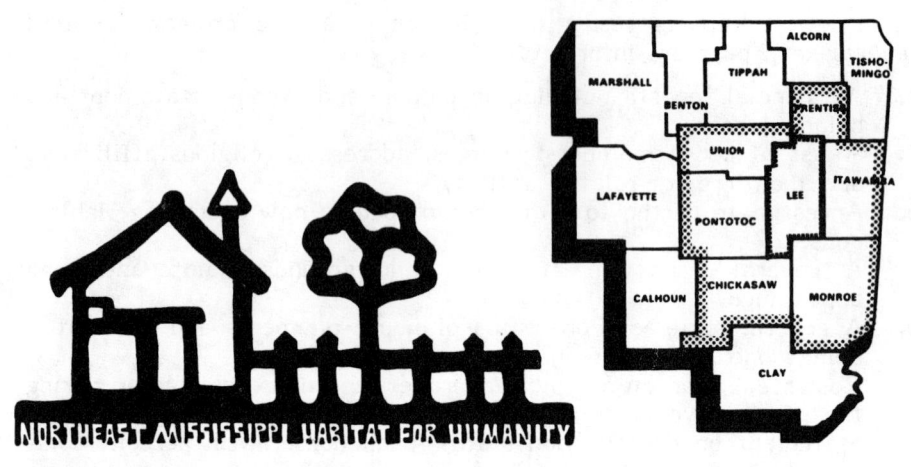

Adopted Logo NEMSHFH   *Target Service Area*

Date: March 11, 1985
Name of Project: Northeast Mississippi Habitat for Humanity
Business Address: P.O. Box 1053, Tupelo, Mississippi 38802
Telephone: 601/844-8989
Three Principals: Alice Gordon   Rev. Davis Carothers
                    636 Highland Cir.   P.O. Box 66
                    Tupelo MS 38801   Belden MS 38826

                    David Crews
                    P.O. Box 1053
                    Tupelo MS 38802

Please attach a list of your Board of Directors. Include names, addresses, religious affiliation, and their project-related responsibility.

Incorporated? Yes.   When? 11/29/84.   Where? Mississippi.
Tax Exempt?   No. Application for exemption has been made.

(Copies of Corporate Charter, By-Laws, and Tax Exemption would help.)

Answer the following in the spirit of a self-evaluation, as well as a communication of what you are to those who wish to know.

1. **STATE THE PURPOSE OF YOUR ORGANIZATION.**

   The purpose of Northeast Mississippi Habitat for Humanity (hereafter referred to as NEMSHFH) is found in the preamble of our by-laws, as quoted here:

   "NEMSHFH, Incorporated shall seek to sponsor specific projects in habitat globally, starting with the construction of modest but adequate housing, and to associate with other groups functioning with purposes consistent with those listed below, namely:

   A. To witness to the Gospel of Jesus Christ throughout the world, working in cooperation with God's people in need to create a better habitat in which to live and work.

   B. To work in co-operation with other agencies and groups which have a kindred purpose.

   C. To witness to the Gospel of Jesus Christ through loving acts and the spoken and written word.

   D. To enable an expanding number of persons from all walks of life to participate in this ministry."

2. **EXPRESS YOUR VISION OF HABITAT FOR YOUR COMMUNITY, IN GENERAL LONG-RANGE TERMS, AND IN SPECIFIC TERMS. INCLUDE YOUR SPECIFIC OBJECTIVES FOR THE NEXT FIVE YEARS (WHEN, WHERE, HOW, AS WELL AS WHAT) AND THE MOTIVATIONS, PHILOSOPHY, OR BELIEF WHICH CAUSES YOU TO UNDERTAKE SUCH A TASK.**

   Long- and Short-Range Goals:

   The ultimate long-range goal of NEMSHFH is to eliminate poverty housing in the world as a witness to the Gospel of Jesus Christ. This goal will be accomplished by cooperating with Habitat International in its program toward that end. That vision will be implemented practically by beginning in Lee County, Mississippi, and the adjacent counties of Prentiss, Itawamba, Monroe, Pontotoc, Union, and Chickasaw.

   Our specific objectives for the next five years:
   (1) To involve the churches in the area by speakers in the pulpit; Sunday School; mission groups; and men's, women's, and youth groups. Also, to encourage the formation of work teams from individual churches, and to promote Habitat as a worthy recipient of local mission funds.
   (2) To involve the extensive industrial/business community by presentations to decision makers, requesting labor and material donations.
   (3) To involve civic groups via the same means for involving the

churches.

(4) The response of the above groups and the availability of funds will determine the exact number of houses we are capable of building per year. We anticipate no less than four houses will be begun in 1985, with as many begun in 1986. We anticipate a minimum of five houses per year thereafter.

(5) We anticipate also being a resource group for other Habitat projects which may be organized within the Northeast Mississippi counties.

(6) We anticipate the possibility of a project director being hired to coordinate activities within the first three years.

Motivations:

Our motivations in becoming involved in the Habitat vision are varied, but fall under our individual responses to the Gospel of Jesus Christ. We believe in putting feet, hands, hearts, heads, and resources behind our prayers and because of our faith. The greatest commandment is to love God; the second, to love others as ourselves. John reminds us not to just talk about love but to put it into action in meeting of the needs of others. Christ expressed the concern and the identification of God with those who are in poverty situations by His parable of the sheep and goats. We see ourselves as "doing it unto the least of these," His brethren.

3. HOW IS YOUR PROJECT FINANCED NOW? HOW DO YOU SEE DEVELOPING A FINANCIAL BASE IN THE FUTURE?

Our local organization has obtained an initial grant of $15,000 from Create, Incorporated, a local foundation supporting community development endeavors. Also, a local area newspaper, the *Northeast Mississippi Daily Journal*, has contributed $3,000 to our project. We have successfully raised over $2,000 in personal contributions and plan an aggressive fund-raising campaign to include a "Habitat Sunday" at local churches and solicitation from other area organizations and citizens. We feel that through our initial success and our planned activities we will be on a sound financial basis within the next few years.

4. WHAT SAFEGUARDS DO YOU HAVE TO ENSURE THAT MONEY AND PROPERTY RAISED FOR YOUR PROJECT WILL ALL REACH ITS INTENDED USE?

Accounting procedures have been established for the receipt of funds and include dual control over all disbursements. All persons having signatory power on the bank accounts are to be bonded. Also, a treasurer's report is prepared and presented to the Board of Directors at each monthly meeting. Additionally, a planned, annual independent audit by a local CPA firm is to be performed at the end of each fiscal year. All work performed by members of our organization is to be strictly on a volunteer basis.

5. WHAT RESOURCES (OTHER THAN FINANCIAL) ARE PRESENTLY AVAILABLE TO YOUR PROJECT, INCLUDING EXPERIENCE, CONTACTS, EXPERTISE, OR OTHER ASSISTANCE YOU CAN COUNT ON NOW?

NEMSHFH's greatest resources are a strong organizational structure, an energetic volunteer membership with wide-ranging experience and expertise, the committed support of various public and private agencies, and the established administrative services of CREATE, Incorporated, a local human resource foundation.

The organizational structure is comprised of a sixteen-member Board of Directors and six standing committees. A look at the membership of the board reveals that a broad cross-section of the community is involved, with professions and occupations representing expertise that is invaluable to the success of NEMSHFH. All board members actively use their expertise in serving, along with other volunteers, on standing committees (Family Relations, Site Selection, Building, Finance, and Development).

NEMSHFH has received the support of various local public and private agencies. Among these are:
(1) LIFT, Inc., a community action agency.
(2) The Salvation Army.
(3) Lee County Ministerial Association.
(4) Tennessee Valley Authority, home planning and efficiency department.
(5) Homebuilders Association, an association of over 50 local contractors and construction material suppliers.
(6) CREATE, Inc., a local human resource foundation.

CREATE is providing strong assistance. In addition to financial support and its executive director serving on the NEMSHFH Board, CREATE serves as an administrative base, processing all donations under its own umbrella non-profit tax-exempt status and maintaining records. Also, a local business, the Stewart C. Irby Co., has pledged the donation of all electrical wiring and circuitry for Habitat homes.

A local professional writer is establishing and editing a statewide Habitat newsletter which will contain news concerning, and provide a vehicle for donations to, all Mississippi Habitat projects. The area newspaper, the *Northeast Mississippi Daily Journal*, will publish this at no cost to the Habitat projects. The headquarters of the National Federation for Decency is providing word- and data-processing capabilities for maintaining the newsletter mailing list.

Finally, the Tupelo and Lee County area has a rich history and tradition of community service. Through the proper channeling of information and the soliciting of support, the NEMSHFH can capture this demonstrated spirit of civic pride and commitment.

6. HOW DO YOU HOPE THAT HABITAT FOR HUMANITY CAN ASSIST YOU? WHAT SPECIFIC INPUT FROM THE OUTSIDE DO YOU SEE AS NECESSARY TO GET YOUR PROJECT UNDERWAY, OR KEEP IT GOING?

At this time we anticipate that Habitat International will function primarily as a resource center, providing information on how other affiliates have approached problems that we may encounter, and for which we have little or no background for handling. We do not anticipate requiring many resources beyond that.

7. WHAT CRITERIA WILL YOU USE IN CHOOSING THE PLACES YOU WILL SERVE?

(1) The cost of the land will have a tremendous effect on the project in the initial stage because of limited funds.
(2) It will be important that the title is clear or can be cleared within a reasonable length of time.
(3) Owner-occupied locations with applicant rankings high on the family selection criteria will be given special consideration initially.
(4) Availability of utilities, ingress and egress, and physical condition of the site will be considered.

8. WHAT CRITERIA WILL BE USED IN CHOOSING THE PEOPLE YOU WILL SERVE?

These family selection criteria have been adopted by NEMSHFH's Family Relations Committee:
(1) Houses will be built only for the families who do not presently have adequate housing and who do not have the financial means to build, according to current conventional means.
(2) Family size and need will be considered. When all other priorities are equally met, the family with the greatest number of individuals will be chosen.
(3) Family size and composition will be important factors. Unless a special exception is made, a family unit:
    a. Shall not exceed the capacity of the house.
    b. Must fit the guidelines of not more than two persons per bedroom.
    c. Shall not include an unwed couple.
(4) Applicants must show visible evidence of concern for proper maintenance of present living quarters.
(5) Only families with a good reputation for honesty will be selected.

(6) Applicants shall exhibit good moral character.

(7) Applicants shall agree to commit a reasonable amount of time (with a miniumum of 500 hours per family), energy, and other personal resources to the finishing of their house. Families are expected to assist in the construction of Habitat houses however possible. This may include clearing the lot, painting, helping with actual construction, providing food for workers, or other activities.

(8) Applicants must be able to show a stable employment record.

(9) Applicants must be able to demonstrate a history of financial responsibility. Credit references will be requested and verified.

(10) Families chosen for homes must save and pay to Habitat a down payment of $500. This payment must be made within six months of notification of selection, or one month prior to occupancy, whichever comes first.

(11) Families must demonstrate the financial resources to pay the minimum monthly payment on a regular basis. The exact payment will be determined on an individual basis.

(12) A combination deed of trust/promissory note agreement will be made with the owners. The first mortgage on the property will be for the selling price of the home. A second mortgage will be placed on the property for the amount of the difference between the selling price and the appraised market value. This second mortgage (and accompanying promissory note) dissolves an equal percentage each year over a ten-year period for new construction. The second mortgage dissolves totally at the end of the specified period.

(13) NEMSHFH will have the first option to buy back a house if the owners want to sell it during the life of the first mortgage. If NEMSHFH wishes to buy it, the owner will sell it to Habitat at no more than the original cost, plus the difference between the original appraised market value and the market value at the time of selling, less any remaining mortgage value.

(14) The family is responsible for maintenance and repairs of the house from the time of occupancy. The family is also responsible for taxes and insurance, which are paid on a monthly basis in addition to house payments.

(15) Lot size will meet governmental unit regulations. Houses will meet applicable code standards. Any additions or other buildings added to the original house are prohibited during the term of the mortgage unless approved by the Habitat board in advance.

(16) Families are encouraged to contribute to the work of Habitat in a spontaneous manner. This may include money, labor, input at meetings, and so forth. When all other criteria for selection are met equally by two or more families, the one most active in the work will be chosen.

(17) If more than one family meets all these guidelines on a fairly equal basis, the family who was first to submit their application shall be chosen.

9. WHAT DO YOU HOPE TO ACCOMPLISH FOR AND WITH THE PEOPLE YOU WILL SERVE?

NEMSHFH hopes to:
(1) Alleviate their suffering due to inadequate housing.
(2) Serve as witnesses to/with them of the Gospel of Jesus Christ.
(3) Teach homemaking and gardening skills where lacking.
(4) Link them, where needed, with information/resources to help in everyday living, whether their need be physical, mental, social, or spiritual.

10. HOW ARE THE PEOPLE YOU ARE WORKING WITH INVOLVED IN THE DECISION-MAKING PROCESS?

At this time, we have had few social inroads into the strata of society we anticipate serving. As we publicize the availability of applications and begin to get a pool of persons that are interested, we will expand our committees to include these persons, who will have full voice and vote.

11. DO YOU REQUIRE "SWEAT EQUITY" FROM RECIPIENTS?

Yes, with a minimum of 500 hours per family.

12. WILL RECIPIENTS OWN THEIR HOUSES OR APARTMENTS? THEIR LAND?

Yes, subject to normal mortgage arrangements.

13. WHAT COMMUNITY SUPPORT AND/OR DEVELOPMENT SERVICES WILL YOU PROVIDE?

As we move into the program, we anticipate developing programs, services, and resources for the recipients based on their particular needs. We see ourselves as partners with them in not only meeting their housing needs, but also in connecting them with available resources in other areas--food, clothing, medical, etc.

14. THE AFFILIATE COUNCIL AND HABITAT BOARD OF DIRECTORS STRONGLY BELIEVE THAT ALL AFFILIATES SHOULD TITHE THEIR INCOME TO THE INTERNATIONAL MINISTRY OF HABITAT, INCLUDING THE EXPENSE OF THE AFFILIATE COORDINATOR POSITION. WHAT IS YOUR BOARD'S THINKING ON THIS IMPORTANT MATTER?

At the time our organization formed, it was understood by one of our members who was in attendance at the Amarillo meeting that tithing of both house payments and all contributions was made mandatory by the International Board. Support has been expressed because of the effective ministry we know Habitat does internationally.

15. SOME GOOD RESEARCH INTO THE NEEDS OF THE COMMUNITY CAN BE HELPFUL IN DEVELOPING A HABITAT PROJECT. WHAT IS THE POPULATION OF THE AREA YOU INTEND TO SERVE? OTHER INDICATORS OF HOUSING NEEDS WOULD BE HELPFUL.

	Square Miles	Population White	Population Black	Population Other	Housing Units
Primary Area					
County:					
LEE	418	45,227	11,651	550	21,373*
Secondary Area					
Counties:					
CHICKASAW	506	11,383	6,434	194	6,346
ITAWAMBA	541	19,383	1,264	176	7,640
MONROE	769	25,544	10,813	277	13,247
PONTOTOC	501	17,618	3,259	211	8,148
PRENTISS	418	21,383	2,590	182	8,951
UNION	422	18,701	3,000	180	8,265
Totals:	3,575	159,052	39,011	1,770	73,970

*A Lee County Council of Government's report in 1979 indicated that as much as 20 percent of Lee County homes are substandard.
Source: "Mississippi Statistical Abstract" (Mississippi State University).

16. DO YOU FORESEE ANY PROBLEM IN YOUR FURNISHING SEMI-ANNUAL PROGRESS REPORTS TO HABITAT, SERVING ON HABITAT BOARDS OR COMMITTEES, HOSTING OCCASIONAL VISITATIONS TO YOUR PROJECTS?

Progress reports and hosting visitations pose no problems. Decisions about serving on Habitat boards or committees are solely dependent on the individual NEWSHFH director.

17. PLEASE MAKE ANY ADDITIONAL COMMENTS ABOUT YOUR PROJECT THAT YOU THINK WOULD BE OF INTEREST TO HABITAT'S BOARD OF DIRECTORS. A BRIEF PROGRESS REPORT WOULD BE MOST HELPFUL.

Attached you will find copies of newspaper articles which have appeared in the *Northeast Mississippi Daily Journal* concerning NEMSHFH organizing efforts. At the time of appearance at the Salem County Habitat International meeting, we will make a full progress report, and will present copies of the new statewide Habitat newsletter.

SUBMISSION OF THIS APPLICATION APPROVED THIS 11TH DAY OF MARCH 1985, BY VOTE OF THE NORTHEAST MISSISSIPPI HABITAT FOR HUMANITY, INCORPORATED BOARD OF DIRECTORS AT ITS REGULARLY SCHEDULED MEETING AT FIRST UNITED METHODIST CHURCH, TUPELO, MISSISSIPPI.

/s/Alice Gordon
President

/s/Davis Carothers
Vice-President

/s/David Sparks
Secretary

/s/Charles Penson
Treasurer

EXCERPTS FROM ARTICLES OF INCORPORATION AND BY-LAWS

The distinctive elements of a non-profit Habitat for Humanity program include the purposes in its Articles of Incorporation and the Preamble in its By-Laws. They are reproduced below. The other elements of Incorporation and By-Laws must follow state requirements.

The corporation is organized for the following purposes:

(a) To implement the Gospel of Jesus Christ throughout the United States and around the world by working with economically disadvantaged people to help them create a better human habitat in which to live and work.

(b) To cooperate with other charitable organizations, through grants and otherwise, which are working to develop a better habitat for economically disadvantaged people.

(c) To communicate the Gospel of Jesus Christ by means of the spoken word, and by distribution of Bibles and other Christian literature.

(d) To receive, maintain and accept, as assets of the corporation, any property, whether real, personal or mixed, by way of gift, bequest, devise or purchase from any person, firm, trust or corporation, to be held, administered and disposed of in accordance with and pursuant to the provisions of this Charter of Incorporation; but no gift, bequest, devise or purchase of any such property shall be received or made and accepted if it is conditioned or limited in such manner as shall require the disposition of income or principal to any organization other than a "charitable organization" or for any purpose other than "charitable purposes" within the respective meanings of such quoted terms as defined in Articles VIII and IX, or which would jeopardize the Federal Income Tax exemption of this corporation pursuant to Section 501 (c)(3) of the Internal Revenue Code of 1954, as now in force or acts in amendment thereof or substitution therefor.

BY-LAWS OF HABITAT FOR HUMANITY, INC.

Preamble

Habitat for Humanity, Incorporated shall seek to sponsor specific projects in habitat development globally, starting with the construction of modest but adequate housing, and to associate with other groups functioning with purposes consistent with those listed below, namely:

A. To witness to the Gospel of Jesus Christ throughout the world by working in cooperation with God's people in need to create a better habitat in which to live and work.

B. To work in cooperation with other agencies and groups which

have a kindred purpose.
C. To witness to the Gospel of Jesus Christ through loving acts and the spoken and written word.
D. To enable an expanding number of persons from all walks of life to participate in this ministry.

APPENDIX A: COMPLETE LISTING OF MATERIALS AVAILABLE THROUGH HABITAT

The following is a consolidated listing of all Habitat materials, many of which have been mentioned previously in this *Manual*. These, and other related titles in the second section, can be ordered through **Habitat for Humanity, Inc., Habitat and Church Streets, Americus, Georgia 31709-3498** (telephone: 912/924-6935).

Following this listing are three sample house plans (Appendix B) which Habitat for Humanity has used for low-cost housing constructed. A collection of house plans is also available through Habitat (see below). Further sources of information on low-cost, energy-efficient housing can be found in Appendix C.

HABITAT MATERIALS
(Prices are postpaid.)

Books

Bokotola by Millard Fuller. (1977) $4.95
   The story of the first housing project in Zaire and the events leading up to the creation of Habitat for Humanity.

Cotton Patch Evidence by Dallas Lee. (1971) $3.50
   The story of Clarence Jordan and Koinonia Farm, where Habitat for Humanity was born.

Habitat Affiliate Operations Manual edited by Ted Swisher. (1985) $10.00
   Details about the ongoing questions and functions of a Habitat affiliate. (Mimeograph.)

Kingdom Building: Essays from the Grassroots of Habitat edited by David Johnson Rowe and Robert William Stevens. (1984) $4.95

In-depth essays from the experience of Habitat partners--for leaders of local projects.

Love in the Mortar Joints by Millard Fuller and Diane Scott. (1980) $4.95
The more complete story of Millard Fuller's personal pilgrimage and the remarkable ministry of Habitat for Humanity through 1981.

No More Shacks! by Millard Fuller. (forthcoming early 1986)
The continuing story of Habitat for Humanity and its campaign to eliminate poverty housing.

Audio Visuals

Film (16mm): "Shelter of God's Love" (29 min.). $25.00 rental.

Audiocassettes: "The Economics of Jesus" (Millard Fuller), "Envisioning" (David Rowe). $3.50 each.

Slide Shows: "Celebrate Habitat," "Celebrate Habitat Around the World," "Julia Doesn't Live Here Any More," "Love in the Mortar Joints II." $25.00 each.

Videocassettes: "Celebrate Habitat," "Habitat Oyee," "Righteous Economics," "Shelter of God's Love," "World in Need: Opportunity to Share." $25.00 each.

(Slide shows and videocassettes can be sent on 30-day consignment)

Informational Packets

"Building a Workcamp." Complimentary illustrated booklet on organizational techniques for developing a successful workcamp at a local project.

"Foundation and Fundraising Information." A packet of information to assist the affiliated project in applying for grants from foundations. Sample proposals are included, as well as other fundraising ideas and information. $5.00

"Media Resource Guide." This publication, designed to demonstrate how the media work and think, will assist your group in using the media to spread the vision of Habitat. $5.00

"Miscellaneous House Plans." A collection of floor plans used by the Americus Habitat for Humanity project. Working drawings are available on request. $2.00

"Public Relations How-to Manual." Complimentary guide to the all-important field of public relations.

"Speakers' Resource Packet." Up-to-date information on all sponsored and affiliated projects, promotional and inspirational materials, with speakers' tips. Includes two videocassette tapes. $7.00

OTHER RELATED TITLES AVAILABLE THROUGH HABITAT
(Please add $2.00 *per total order* to cover postage and handling.)

From the Ground Up by John N. Cole and Charles Wing (founder of Cornerstones, the Wing School of Shelter Technology, Maine). (1976) $14.45
> Leads you through the process of designing and building a post-industrial home, stressing community resources and relations, and careful utilization of materials with little waste.

From the Walls In by Charles Wing. (1979) $14.45
> Various techniques, facts, and figures that are helpful for remodeling and "retrofitting" an older home.

The Grass Roots Fund Raising Book: How to Raise Money in Your Community by Joan Flanagan. (1982) $9.00
> The mechanics of raising money are all here--how, when, and how much to ask people to donate, including sample fundraising ideas.

Modern Carpentry by Willis H. Wagner. (1983) $21.00 in hardcover.
> A colorful, easy-to-understand encyclopedia of authoritative and up-to-date information on building materials and construction methods, covering all aspects of light frame construction.

New Life for Old Dwellings by Gerald Sherwood (U.S. Department of Agriculture). (1979) $6.50
> The appraisal section of this handbook presents a systematic approach for inspecting a woodframe building and evaluating the information. The rehabilitation portion is an especially useful guide for the planning and successful completion of any structure.

The Successful Volunteer Organization: Getting Started and Getting Results in Nonprofit, Charitable, Grass Roots, and Community Groups by Joan Flanagan. (1981) $13.95
> Joan--a nationally recognized independent consultant on fund-raising, management, and public relations for non-profit groups--

wrote this book to help non-profits establish organizations which their communities seek so much that fundraising becomes a pleasure! Offers practical advice on how to operate effectively and efficiently.

APPENDIX B: SAMPLE HOUSE PLANS

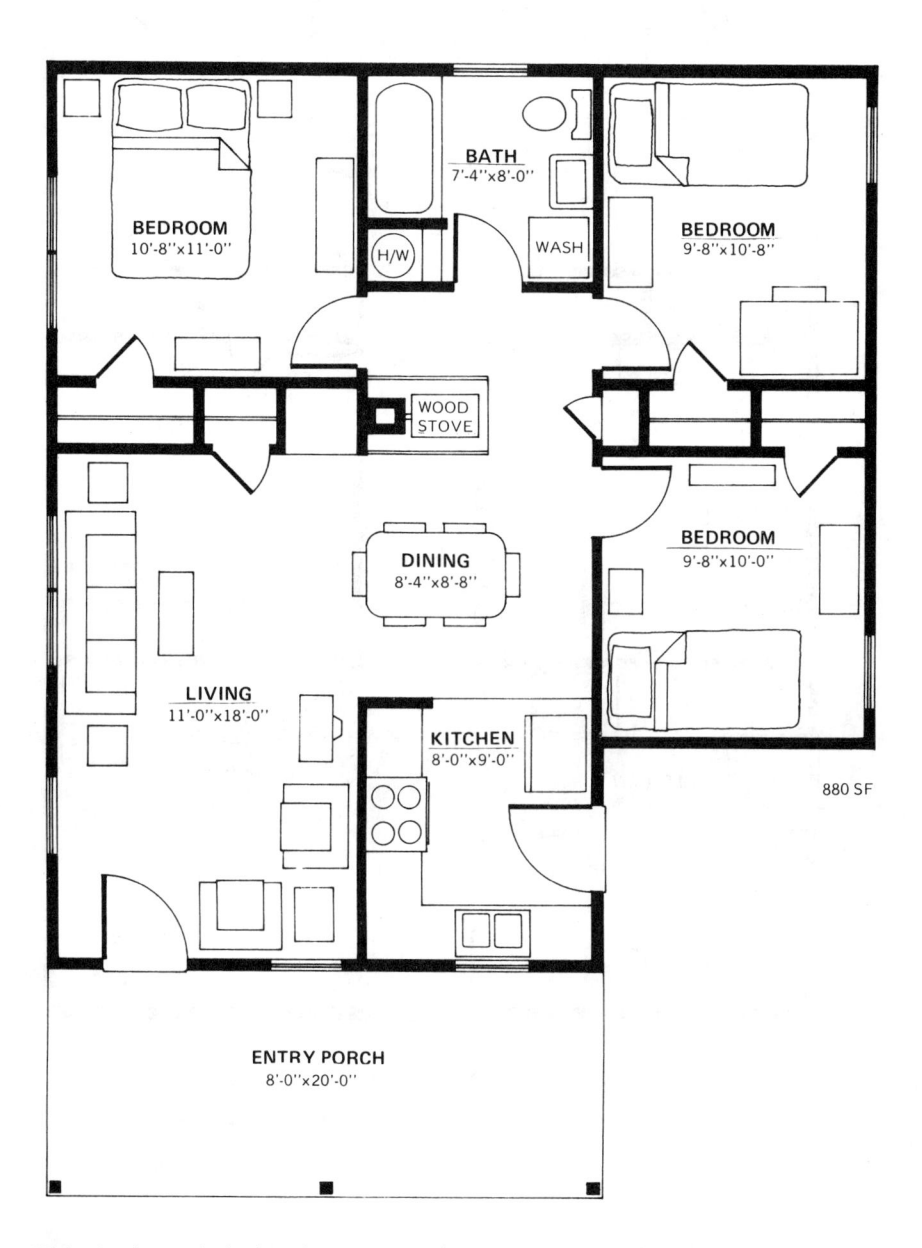

This L-shaped design breaks up the monotony of a simple rectangular plan. The L-shape increases the material and labor costs slightly.

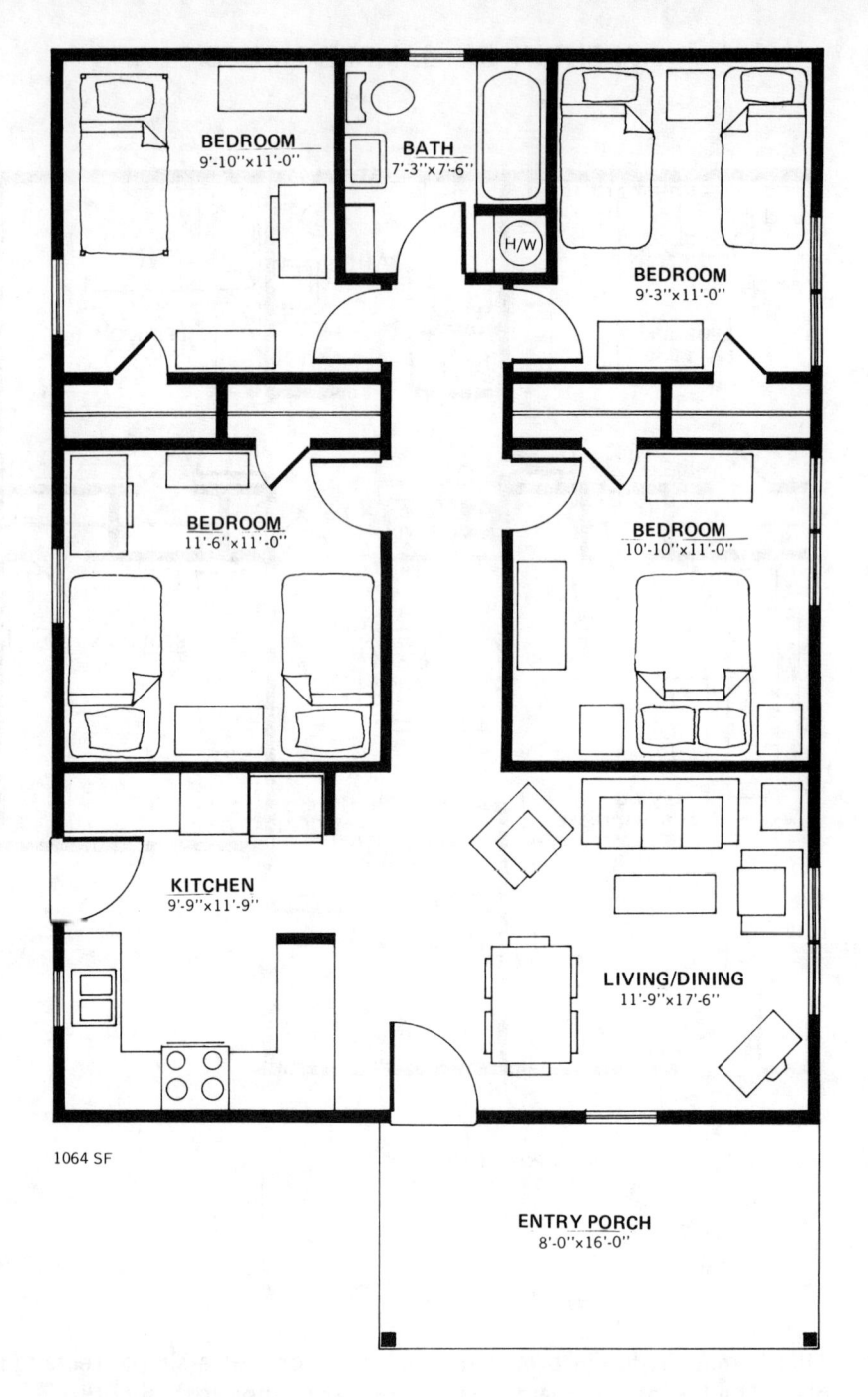

This simple, efficient four-bedroom design is suitable for any situation with an appropriate lot.

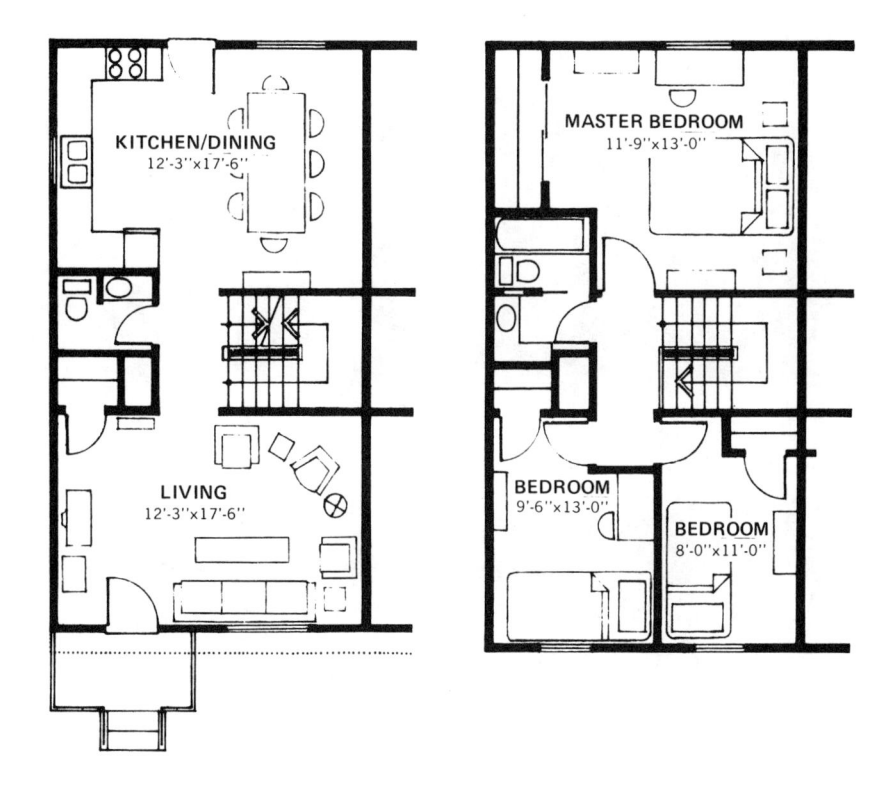

This plan was designed for Paterson Habitat. While the square footage is somewhat large for a three-bedroom Habitat house and there are 1½ baths, these are almost essential elements for a narrow, two-story, urban building.

APPENDIX C: FURTHER SOURCES OF INFORMATION ON LOW-COST, ENERGY-EFFICIENT HOUSING

Sources of information on low-cost, energy-efficient housing design are so numerous that it is hard to know where to begin. Furthermore, new techniques are constantly being tried and new information becoming available. We have, therefore, included only selected publications and community services here, including some periodicals which are continuously updating their information with each issue. (Prices quoted are current at the time of publication. It is always a good idea to verify price, availability, and shipping and handling charges before ordering. We have included as many telephone numbers as possible to facilitate that task.) Unless otherwise noted, all publications are paperbound. (Six other titles are also listed in second section of Appendix A.)

Construction and Design

Anderson, Bruce with Michael Riordan. *The Solar Home Book: Heating, Cooling and Designing with the Sun.* 1976 (Brick House Publishing Co., 3 Main Street, Andover, MA 01810 [617/475-9568], $14.95). A basic book on the fundamentals of solar design and energy conservation, written in straightforward, non-technical language for architects, solar advocates and homeowners alike.

Booth, Don with Jonathan Booth and Peg Boyles. *Sun/Earth Buffering and Superinsulation.* 1983 (Rodale Press for Community Builders, 33 East Minor Street, Emmaus, PA 18049 [215/967-5171], $12.95). Professional, state-of-the-art information is shared by an award-winning solar pioneer in this clear, concise and highly readable book.

Bruyère, Christian and Robert Inwood. *In Harmony with Nature.* Revised edition 1979 (Sterling Publishing Co., 2 Park Avenue, New York, NY 10016 [212/532-7160], $8.95. How to construct sturdy and pleasing shelter while living close to the land.

Campbell, Stu. *The Underground House Book*. 1980 (Garden Way Publishing, Schoolhouse Road, Pownal, VT 05261 [802/823-5811], $10.95). Facts on financing, earth stresses, lighting and humidity control--everything needed in considering the underground home.

Carmody, John and Raymond Sterling. *Earth Sheltered Housing Design*. 2nd ed. 1985 (Van Nostrand Reinhold, 135 West 50th Street, New York, NY 10020 [212/265-8700], $17.50). This revised edition of an earlier study by the Underground Space Center, University of Minnesota, offers a wealth of information on site planning, ground conditions, solar energy, vegetation, building form and layout. Sections also cover insulation, waterproofing, building codes and zoning ordinances.

Clark, Sam. *Designing and Building Your Own Home Your Own Way*. 1978 (Houghton Mifflin Co., 2 Park Street, Boston, MA 01803 [617/725-5000], $12.70). Whether building yourself or hiring professionals, this manual helps you retain control of the project technically, financially and aesthetically. Photographs of many owner-designed and owner-built houses are included with explanatory text on the essentials of engineering principles, designing for family needs and estimating time and money.

Crowther, Richard L. *Affordable Passive Solar Homes*. 1983 (SciTech Publishing, P.O. Box 587, Denver, CO 80224 [303/355-7202], $24.00). Following a general discussion of passive solar design which emphasizes the author's supportive views for a conserving lifestyle, the second section contains 49 houses for cold climates that are displayed on two-page spreads. Designs range from 242 to 1,416 square feet (including some duplexes and townhouses) with conceptual plans, perspective sketches and cross-sections.

Edelhart, Mike. *The Handbook of Earth Shelter Design*. 1982 (Dolphin Books, Doubleday & Co., 245 Park Avenue, New York, NY 10167 [212/953-4561], $11.95). Documents in clear, non-technical language the environmental advantages and energy savings of underground housing with a detailed description of soil characteristics, thermal conductivity, ventilation and humidity control, structural factors and methods, as well as siting. Includes complete resources listing.

Hibsman, Dan. *Your Affordable Solar Home*. 1984 (Random House for Sierra Club Books, 400 Hahn Road, Westminster, MD 21157 [301/848-1900], $7.95). Describes six designs built for $20,000 or less, averaging 700 square feet, as the result of a 1980 design contest sponsored by the city of Cotati, California.

Kern, Barbara and Ken. *The Owner-Built Pole Frame House*. 1981 (Charles Scribner's Sons, 597 Fifth Avenue, New York, NY 10017 [212/486-2700], $4.95). A well-proven structural principle that is cheaper, stronger and uses less lumber.

_____, Ken. *The Owner-Built Home.* 1975 (Charles Scribner's Sons, 597 Fifth Avenue, New York, NY 10017 [212/486-2700], $8.95). A how-to-do-it book on a wide variety of building techniques, including energy-saving, as alternatives to contractor-built houses. Innovative yet sensible ideas.

Leckie, Jim, Gil Masters, Harry Whitehouse and Lily Young. *More Other Homes and Garbage: Designs for Self-Sufficient Living.* 1981 (Random House for Sierra Club Books, 400 Hahn Road, Westminster, MD 21157 [301/848-1900], $14.95). A revised and updated version of a previous title, this is a good introductory reference to the subject of energy and building. Includes, among other topics, alternative architecture, solar heating, waste systems and water supply, as well as regional climatic charts and sectional annotated bibliographies.

Maine Audubon Society and Maine Bureau of Vocational Education. *Superinsulated Construction.* 1984 (Maine Audubon Society, 118 Route 1, Falmouth, ME 04105 [207/781-2330], $4.00). Using detailed drawings, explains the basic concepts of superinsulation such as high insulation levels, vapor barriers, infiltration control, solar gain and high internal heat gain. A listing of the best resources are included at the end of each chapter.

Metz, Don. *Superhouse.* 1981 (Garden Way Publishing, Schoolhouse Road, Pownal, VT 05261 [802/823-5811], $12.95). The three different approaches to energy-efficient design--earth-sheltered, superinsulated and double envelope--are explained with major advantages and disadvantages examined. An in-depth comparison of the contending design principles, the final section introduces the superhouse hybrid incorporating the best of the three.

_____, ed. *The Compact House Book: 33 Prizewinning Designs, 1,000 Sq. Ft. or Less.* 1983 (Garden Way Publishing, Schoolhouse Road, Pownal, VT 05261 [802/823-5811], $14.95). A selection of the top entries in a national compact-house competition, designs include floor plans, wall sections, costs, and building and structural materials.

Milne, Len. "Suitable for Framing--The Larsen Truss: Superinsulation Made Simple." *Harrowsmith* (Camden East, Ontario, Canada), No. 60, April/May 1985, pp. 44-51. Describes an increasingly popular superinsulation system among the growing ranks of the owner-builder or renovator. (Information packet available for $15 from Sunscape Builders Ltd., 9924 152 Street, Edmonton, Alberta T5P 1X7, Canada.)

Miner, Robert, ed. and staff of The Mother Earth News. *Mother's Homebuilding and Shelter Guide.* 1983. (The Mother Earth News, P.O. Box 70, Hendersonville, NC 28791 [704/693-0211], $12.95). This collection of articles published over the last decade describes the low-cost benefits of solar, earth-sheltered, underground and log houses, with color photos, schematics and special construction tips.

McClintock, Mike. *Alternative Housebuilding.* 1985 (Rodale Press, 33 East Minor Street, Emmaus, PA 18049 [215/967-5171], $32.95 in hardcover). Focuses on some new and proven building systems based on pole foundations, rammed-earth walls and earth sheltering, as well as traditional systems now enjoying widepsread revivals--log building, timber framing and building with adobe, stone or cordwood. 300 diagrams with resource lists.

McGrath, Ed. *The Superinsulated House: A Working Guide for Owner-Builders and Architects.* 1982 (That New Publishing, 1525 Eielson Street, Fairbanks, AK 99701 [907/452-3007], $11.95). The basic principles of superinsulation for cold climates are explained in easy-to-understand terms and through numerous illustrations.

NCAT. *House Plan for Cold Climates.* Revised 1985 (National Center for Appropriate Technology, P.O. Box 3838, Butte, MT 59702 [406/494-4572], $75 first set). Complete 15-page set of construction blueprints for the site-built, three-bedroom, ranch-style design in use in the Montana Superinsulation Project. Contact NCAT for descriptive literature and a listing of other publications on superinsulation and conservation.

Northeast Utilities. *The Solar Home Planbook, 1984.* 1984 (Northeast Utilities, P.O. Box 270, Hartford, CT 06141, no charge). Six different styles, prepared by solar-experienced architectural firms in the northeast, include floor plans, cross-sections, available options, siting information, and performance and operational data. Working drawings available for $50 each ($25 each for Northeast Utilities' customers).

Olkowski, Helga and Bill, Tom Javits and the Farallones Institute staff. *The Integral Urban House: Self-Reliant Living in the City.* 1979 (Random House for Sierra Club Books, 400 Hahn Road, Westminster, MD 21157 [301/848-1900], $14.95). Details how an urban dwelling can be made self-reliant--information that can be used anywhere.

Rogers, Marc, Roger Griffith and editors of Garden Way Publishing. *Getting a Roof Over Your Head: Affordable Housing Alternatives.* 1982 (Garden Way Publishing, Schoolhouse Road, Pownal, VT 05261 [802/823-5811], $9.95). Case histories describe how determined and imaginative individuals found ways to afford homes, including houses built from scavenged materials, unwanted houses moved to desirable locations and many other success stories.

Rollwagon, Mary with Susan Taylor and T. Lance Holthusen. *The*

Consumer's Guide to Earth Sheltered Housing: A Step-by-Step Workbook for Prospective Owners. 1983 (Van Nostrand Reinhold, 135 W. 50th Street, New York, NY 10020 [212/265-8700], $25.50). Many examples of designs, and their histories of financing, code-meeting, zoning, ground water problems, builder education and construction techniques.

Roskind, Robert. *Building Your Own House (The First Part: From Foundations to Framing).* 1984 (Ten Speed Press, P.O. Box 7123, Berkeley, CA 94707 [417/845-8414], $25.95). Part of a series from the Owner Builder Center in Berkeley, California, this book is written from the standpoint of the student and provides detailed instructions with answers to some oft-repeated questions. Well illustrated with sample worksheets, schedules and checklists.

Roy, Robert L. *Cordwood Masonry Houses: A Practical Guide for the Owner-Builder.* 1980 (Sterling Publishing Co., 2 Park Avenue, New York, NY 10016 [212/532-7160], $7.95). A step-by-step guide from finding, seasoning and barking the cordwood to analyzing and projecting costs.

_____. *Money-Saving Strategies for the Owner-Builder.* 1981 (Sterling Publishing Co., 2 Park Avenue, New York, NY 10016 [212/532-7160], $7.95). How to build a house with inexpensive materials, labor-saving methods and energy-efficient designs, including options such as the underground house, round house and the homestead.

_____. *Underground Houses: How to Build a Low-Cost Home.* 1979 (Sterling Publishing Co., 2 Park Avenue, New York, NY 10016 [212/532-7160], $6.95). Describes steps in building a subterranean home, including siting, heat, drainage, design, materials and landscaping.

Seddon, Leigh. *Low-Cost Green Lumber Construction.* 1981 (Garden Way Publishing, Schoolhouse Road, Pownal, VT 05261 [802/823-5811], $8.95). A guide for owner-builders in using roughsawn, green, native wood from local sawmills. Covers selection and purchase of wood, stacking and drying, construction techniques and building systems. Includes instructions for a solar kiln, as well as some disadvantages of building green, e.g., window frames.

Sedway Cooke Associates and Sol-Arc. *Retrofit Right: How to Make Your Old House Energy-Efficient.* 1984 (City of Oakland Planning Department, 1 City Hall Plaza, Oakland, CA 94612 [415/273-3941], $8.81 [$9.33 in California]). Provides a step-by-step method to determine which retrofit strategies are most cost-effective, according to the architectural style of a house, family size and whether done by owner or contractor—and, in most cases, details on how to do the job. The solar chapter is an excellent introduction to the basics of retrofitting while blending new work into the old fabric of a house or neighborhood. Although the many fine drawings are representative of Oakland's Bay Area, designs are adaptable to other needs and climates.

Sobon, Jack and Roger Schroeder. *Timber Frame Construction: All About Post-and-Beam Building.* 1984 (Garden Way Publishing, Schoolhouse Road, Pownal, VT 05261 [802/823-5811], $12.95). If you have only dreamed about the beauty of building with timbers, this book will open your eyes. A book for builders as well as those wishing to have the work done for them. Offers the basics of timber framing, how to design for strength and beauty, and how to combine modern tools and time-tested methods.

Standard Homes Plan Service, Inc. *Compact Homes* ($.65), *Economy Homes* ($.75), and *Energy Saving Homes* ($1.25). These three booklets are part of a series of 14 offered to home builders with floor plans and elevations of from 30 to 50 designs in each. Complete working drawings and other construction forms are available for $45 for the first set. Plan booklets may be ordered from Standard Homes, Box 248, Fuquay-Varina, NC 27526-0248 (toll-free 1-800/672-3161 within NC; toll-free 1-800/334-3153 outside NC). Please add $1.00 to total order for postage and handling.

Sterling Publishing Co. *Solar Dwelling Designs.* 1980 (Sterling, 2 Park Avenue, New York, NY 10016 [212/532-7160], $6.95). Source book of 30 passive and active designs. A guide to using a building site as a part of your home, the effects of climate and some technical considerations.

_____. *Woodframe Houses: Construction and Maintenance.* 1981 (Sterling, 2 Park Avenue, New York, NY 10016 [212/532-7160], $8.95). Handbook of information on materials and construction practices, covering concrete and masonry work, framing, sheathing, windows, doors, siding and insulation.

TVA. *Solar Homes Design Portfolio.* 1985 (Tennessee Valley Authority, Division of Conservation and Energy Management, Residential Branch, 3S111-G Missionary Ridge Place, Chattanooga, TN 37402-2801 [Citizen Action Lines: 615/632-4100 in Knoxville area; toll-free 1-800/362-9250 within Tennessee; toll-free 1-800/251-9242 for AL, GA, KY, MS, NC, VA], no charge). Artist renderings and floor plans for 27 designs, ranging from 1,223 to 2,546 square feet, with construction drawings available at extra cost. TVA offers an impressive variety of other free literature on solar energy.

Wade, Alex. *Alex Wade's Guide to Affordable Houses.* 1984 (Rodale Press, 33 East Minor Street, Emmaus, PA 18049 [215/967-5171], $14.95). The author presents ingenious and detailed plans for making new houses affordable, with almost three dozen houses featured.

_____. *A Design and Construction Handbook for Energy-Saving Houses.* 1980 (Rodale Press, 33 East Minor Street, Emmaus, PA 18049 [215/967-5171], $14.95). Describes preparation and construction methods that make use of natural resources and low-cost building techniques. Includes 93 floor plans and elevations.

_____ and Neal Ewenstein. *30 Energy-Efficient Houses... You Can Build.* 1977 (Rodale Press, 33 East Minor Street, Emmaus, PA 18049 [215/967-5171], $12.95). How to build a house that is energy-efficient, solar heated and uses space well. Describes low-cost construction using recycled and easy-maintenance materials, post-and-beam framing and ingenious shortcuts. Designs are balanced between the site-specific and the adaptable.

Watson, Donald. *Designing and Building a Solar Home.* Revised edition. 1985 (Garden Way Publishing, Schoolhouse Road, Pownal, VT 05261 [802/823-5811], $15.95). A practical how-to book that clearly demonstrates how to combine good house design with contemporary solar heating technology.

Wells, Malcolm. *Underground Designs.* 1981 (Brick House Publishing Co., 3 Main Street, Andover, MA 01810 [617/475-9568], $7.95). Plans for homes, as well as offices, institutions and public works, with information on site selection, structural design, waterproofing and insulation, landscaping and dealing with building codes and zoning regulations.

Wing, Charles. *HouseWarming with Charlie Wing.* 1983 (Little, Brown & Company, 200 West Street, Waltham, MA 02154 [617/890-0250], $17.95). Based on the PBS TV program, the book explains all the details of retrofitting for energy efficiency in a clear, well-researched and highly readable manner.

Wolfe, Ralph with Douglas Merrilees and Evelyn Loveday. *Low-Cost Pole Building Construction.* 1980 (Garden Way Publishing, Schoolhouse Road, Pownal, VT 05261 [802/823-5811], $10.95). With a flexibility in site choice and few materials, money-saving plans are presented for homes, barns, garages and other outbuildings.

Other Sources of Help: Periodicals, Networks, Organizations

Alternative Sources of Energy, Inc., 107 South Central Avenue, Milaca, MN 56353 (612/983-6892). The purpose of ASE is to disseminate information on the development and use of renewable energy sources, with special emphasis on information concerning the renewable energy power industry. ASE provides several services: (a) publishes the *Alternative Sources of Energy Magazine* and *Wind Industry News Digest*, as well as books and media; (b) sponsors conferences and seminars; and (c) maintains a specialized energy information and referral service.

Center for Community Development and Preservation, Inc., 18 Hamilton Place, Tarrytown, NY 10591 (914/332-4144). A non-profit, technical assistance and research group, the Center and its affiliate, the Housing Action Council, seek to upgrade and expand the supply of affordable housing. The various programs of the Center and the Council extend to the public and private sectors, developers and property owners, and non-profit and self-help groups. A number of guidebooks on housing and community development issues have been prepared as an outcome of sponsored workshops, covering financing, affordable new housing, and preservation and rehabilitation.

Center for Neighborhood Technology, 570 West Randolph Street, Chicago, IL 60606 (312/454-0126). Along with research/policy development, demonstration projects and training, the Center publishes a variety of materials on self-help neighborhood development issues with emphasis on basic needs such as food, energy and shelter. Their information service, *The Neighborhood Works*, published 12 times a year ($18), includes articles on urban housing throughout the country. Sample copy with recent index available for $2 to cover postage and handling.

Community Economics, Inc., 1904 Franklin Street, Suite 900, Oakland, CA 94612 (415/832-8300). CEI is a non-profit corporation providing technical assistance to community organizations, tenant groups and public agencies in the development, financing and syndication of non-profit and cooperatively owned housing. CEI's work includes projects involving new construction, rehabilitation, historic properties, mobile home parks, tenant conversion and artists' live/work space. CEI is a nationally recognized authority on the development and organization of limited equity housing cooperatives.

Enterprise Foundation, The, 505 American City Building, Columbia, MD 21044 (301/964-1230). Founded in 1982, The Enterprise Foundation is a non-profit, publicly supported organization whose objective is to help the very poor help themselves to decent, livable housing through an expanding network of nationwide, non-profit neighborhood groups. Besides extending small seed money grants and low-interest loans, the Foundation provides assistance in reducing housing costs, obtaining financing and local business support, and establishing job placement agencies and other social services. Its Rehab Work Group publishes a monthly newsletter, *Cost Cuts*, that provides information on reducing construction costs in low-income housing construction and rehabilitation.

Midwest Association of Housing Cooperatives, 343 South Main Street, Room 208, Ann Arbor, MI 48104 (313/994-4314). A non-profit, tax-exempt association, MAHC provides consultation and informational services to its membership, including the bimonthly *MAHC Newsletter*. They have put together a comprehensive reference tool, *Cooperative Housing: A Handbook for Effective Operations*, available for $16.25 postpaid.

McAuley Institute, The, 1320 Fenwick Lane, Suite 600, Silver Spring, MD 20910 (301/588-8110). The Institute was founded in 1982 by the Sisters of Mercy of the Union in response to a perceived lack of adequate housing, especially for women and children. It operates both a technical assistance/consulting service and a short-term Revolving Loan Fund (RLF), both available to qualified non-profit groups or organizations. A resource bank of over 1,700 entries provides information on local, state and national programs, including materials on funding and financing, and serves also as a source of referrals which are often made to other more local organizations.

National Association of Housing Cooperatives, 2501 M Street, N.W., Suite 451, Washington, DC 20037 (202/887-0706). NAHC provides services designed to strengthen housing cooperatives in the way of conferences, training seminars, research and an informational clearinghouse. They publish the *Cooperative Housing Bulletin* and the *Cooperative Housing Journal*, and have other publications on establishing and managing housing cooperatives.

National Low Income Housing Coalition, 1012 14th Street, N.W., Suite 1006, Washington, DC 20005 (202/662-1530). A coalition of individuals and organizations concerned with the housing needs of primarily very low-income people, NLIHC moniters developments and programs, develops policy positions and proposals, and circulates to its members the occasional bulletins, "Memo to Members" and "Call to Action." Its sister organization at the same address--the Low Income Housing Information Service--publishes a monthly newsletter, *Low Income Housing Round Up* ($35), which focuses on what is going on at the federal level affecting low-income housing.

New Shelter, Rodale Press, Inc., 33 East Minor Street, Emmaus, PA 18049 (215/967-5171 or 5141), 9 issues yearly, $10. In-depth coverage of construction alternatives for the homeowner, including energy-saving tips in housing design. Special service departments offer advice on design trends and innovations, new products and test reports, real estate trends and a reader-to-reader column.

Northeast Sun, New England Solar Energy Association and Mid-Atlantic Solar Energy Association, P.O. Box 541, Brattleboro, VT

05301 (802/254-2386). 6 issues yearly. $30 with full association membership. A regional magazine, promoting the understanding and use of solar energy and other renewable energy sources throughout the northeast, with regular features on housing design and construction.

Rain, Center for Urban Education, 3116 North Williams, Portland, OR 97227 (503/249-7218). 6 issues yearly, $18 ($12 for those with incomes under $7,500 a year). Publishes information to help communities and regions become economically self-reliant, leading people to more satisfying lifestyles and building a society that is durable and ecologically sound. Issues feature frequent articles and information on low-cost, cooperative housing.

Shelter Institute, 38 Center Street, Bath, ME 04530 (207/442-7938). Begun in 1974 as the first owner-builder school, the Institute schedules classes year-round with films and workshops for all interested in building their own home. Every aspect of construction is covered, stressing energy conservation. Classes run 90 hours and receive four college credits, VA benefits, and real estate and teacher recertification credits. (Approximately one-third of the students choose renovation of older homes.) An additional one-week course is offered in post-and-beam construction. Two films are available for rental, and on-the-road seminars and weekend workshops offered for builders, realtors and designers. The Institute maintains a tools store ($2 for catalogue) and a comprehensive mail-order service covering books, building materials and drafting supplies (write for free listing).
    Other owner-builder schools include: Cornerstones, 54 Cumberland Street, Brunswick, ME 04011 (207/729-5103), also maintaining a research and development department on energy-efficient building techniques, and the Owner Builder Center, 1824 Fourth Street, Berkeley, CA 94710 (415/848-5950) which also offers leadership training to found other schools--over a dozen now across the country.

Solar Age, Solar Vision, Inc., 7 Church Hill, Harrisville, NH 03450 (603/827-3347). Monthly, $32. Aimed more at the professional, issues include many clearly described and innovative tips on building or remodeling for energy efficiency.

TRANET (Transnational Network for Appropriate/Alternative Technologies), P.O. Box 567, Rangeley, ME 04970 (207/864-2252). A transnational network of, by and for people developing appropriate technologies. Its quarterly newsletter-directory ($30) is a continuing guide to publications, programs and organizations, worldwide. A special pull-out directory in each issue lists groups and periodicals focusing on a specific topic, including, among others, "The Future of Community" and "Self-Help Housing."

The Urban Homesteading Assistance Board, Cathedral House, 1047 Amsterdam Avenue, New York, NY 10025 (212/749-0602). UHAB provides technical assistance to tenant groups, neighborhood organizations and government agencies to address low- and moderate-income housing problems through self-help, self-management, resident control and cooperative ownership. Services, available within New York City as well as around the country, include a "Cooperative Support Program" and a "Homesteader's Handbook" series covering urban management, development and rehab construction.

(Cooperative housing organizations mentioned above are only a selected few; many state and local organizations exist across the country.)

Note: As this edition of the *Manual* goes to press, ITDG/NA is now exploring with the Rocky Mountain Institute appropriate ways of sharing the Institute's pioneering work on saving electricity through one or more publications for those involved in the low-cost housing field. Contact Save Electricity, ITDG/NA, 777 United Nations Plaza, Suite 9A, New York, NY 10017 (212/972-9877) for further details.

DIRECT CREDITS

Many of the contributions to this book, as indicated in the acknowledgements, were made by many different individuals, such that authorship cannot be traced. Yet, there are portions written by specific individuals. These are credited below:

Tom Brooks on "The Nashville Area Habitat's Approach."

Kathy Dupont on "Volunteers--An Important Resource."

William Givens on "Rationale."

Dan Rhema on "The Site Selection Committee."

Harry Sangree on "A Brief History."

Robert William Stevens on "Habitat Visions," "The Habitat Covenant," "Affiliate Tithing," and "Sweat Equity."

Ted Swisher on "Government Funds," "Assessment of Needs," "Inflation," and "The Board of Directors."